CANDLES

MAKING • DECORATING • STYLING

CANDLES

MAKING · DECORATING · STYLING

AN INSPIRED GUIDE TO CREATIVE CANDLES WITH 40 STEP-BY-STEP
PROJECTS AND OVER 325 SPECIALLY COMMISSIONED PHOTOGRAPHS

GLORIA NICOL

southwater

FOR MY MOTHER AND FATHER

AUTHOR'S ACKNOWLEDGEMENTS

I would like to thank Debbie Patterson for her exquisite photography and ability to always bring something extra to every picture, even when working under great pressure; Clare Nicholson for her essential input and patience; Nicky Thompson for making the completion of the book seem a possibility; the designers and makers whose combined talents helped to produce such innovative projects, especially Mary Maguire and Deborah Schneebeli-Morrell for their encouraging telephone conversations and Emma Hardy for always helping out at a minute's notice; John Morgan and Sandra for giving us the run of their homes to provide locations for photography. Finally, a big thank you to all the companies and shops who so kindly and generously gave and loaned such wonderful things for us to photograph.

This edition is published by Southwater, an imprint of Anness Publishing Ltd, Hermes House, 88–89 Blackfriars Road, London SE1 8HA; tel. 020 7401 2077; fax 020 7633 9499

www.southwaterbooks.com; www.annesspublishing.com

If you like the images in this book and would like to investigate using them for publishing, promotions or advertising, please visit our website www.practicalpictures.com for more information.

UK agent: The Manning Partnership Ltd; tel. 01225 478444; fax 01225 478440; sales@manning-partnership.co.uk
UK distributor: Grantham Book Services Ltd; tel. 01476 541080; fax 01476 541061; orders@gbs.tbs-ltd.co.uk
North American agent/distributor: National Book Network; tel. 301 459 3366; fax 301 429 5746; www.nbnbooks.com
Australian agent/distributor: Pan Macmillan Australia; tel. 1300 135 113; fax 1300 135 103; customer.service@macmillan.com.au
New Zealand agent/distributor: David Bateman Ltd; tel. (09) 415 7664; fax (09) 415 8892

Publisher: Joanna Lorenz
Project Editor: Clare Nicholson
Designer: Peter Butler
Special Photography: Debbie Patterson
Step-by-step Photography: Madeleine Brehaut
Production Controller: Wendy Lawson

ETHICAL TRADING POLICY

Because of our ongoing ecological investment programme, you, as our customer, can have the pleasure and reassurance of knowing that a tree is being cultivated on your behalf to naturally replace the materials used to make the book you are holding. For further information about this scheme, go to www.annesspublishing.com/trees

Previously published as *Candles: Making and Displaying*

PUBLISHER'S NOTE

Candles form an essential part of all of the displays in this book. Burning candles are beautiful but can of course be a fire hazard, so please take care at all times to ensure that candles are firmly secured and that lighted candles are never left unattended. An effective flame-resistant spray can be applied to displays though this will not make them fireproof. Where applicable metric and imperial measurements are given. To ensure accurate results, choose only one set of measurements and stick with them throughout a project.

CONTENTS

INTRODUCTION

Before gas and electricity became common sources of power available to everyone, candles were the only source of artificial light. Now, even though no longer a necessity, we still choose to use candles, not only for their decorative qualities but because of something even more special that attracts us to them. Candles have the ability to change the mood of the room, to create an atmosphere and enchant everyone with their flickering beauty.

From the earliest times, candles and tapers were made by dipping rushes into tallow, an animal fat which produces black smoke and an appalling stench when burned. Better-quality candles were made from beeswax but only the rich and the clergy could afford them. It was not until the mid-nineteenth century that the development of stearin as a chemical compound, originally produced from refined fat, changed the technique of candle making, to give longer burning, odour-free candles.

Even though candles today are more likely to burn with a steady flame and are less likely to drip, there might be occasions when you will need to remove spills of wax from furnishings and clothing. To remove wax from carpets and fabrics, allow the wax to cool and harden before tackling the problem. Scrape off what you can with a knife, then iron through a sheet of absorbent paper, which should pick up the rest. For wax on wood, again leave the wax to set, then carefully scrape off the excess, polishing the residue with a soft cloth.

Finally, a word of caution about burning candles as they can, of course, be a fire hazard. Before being lit, all candles should be carefully secured in a holder. The candleholder should be placed a safe distance from any flammable materials. If the candleholder is decorative and part of an arrangement such as dried flowers, or made out of papier mâché, then the candles should be extinguished before they burn down within a few centimetres of the holder.

Above: *These fantastic candles make very stylish and novel presents.*

Opposite: *For Hallowe'en plan a group of these gourds, choosing various colours, textures, shapes and sizes. Select candles which will complement the colours of the gourds.*

CANDLE STYLE

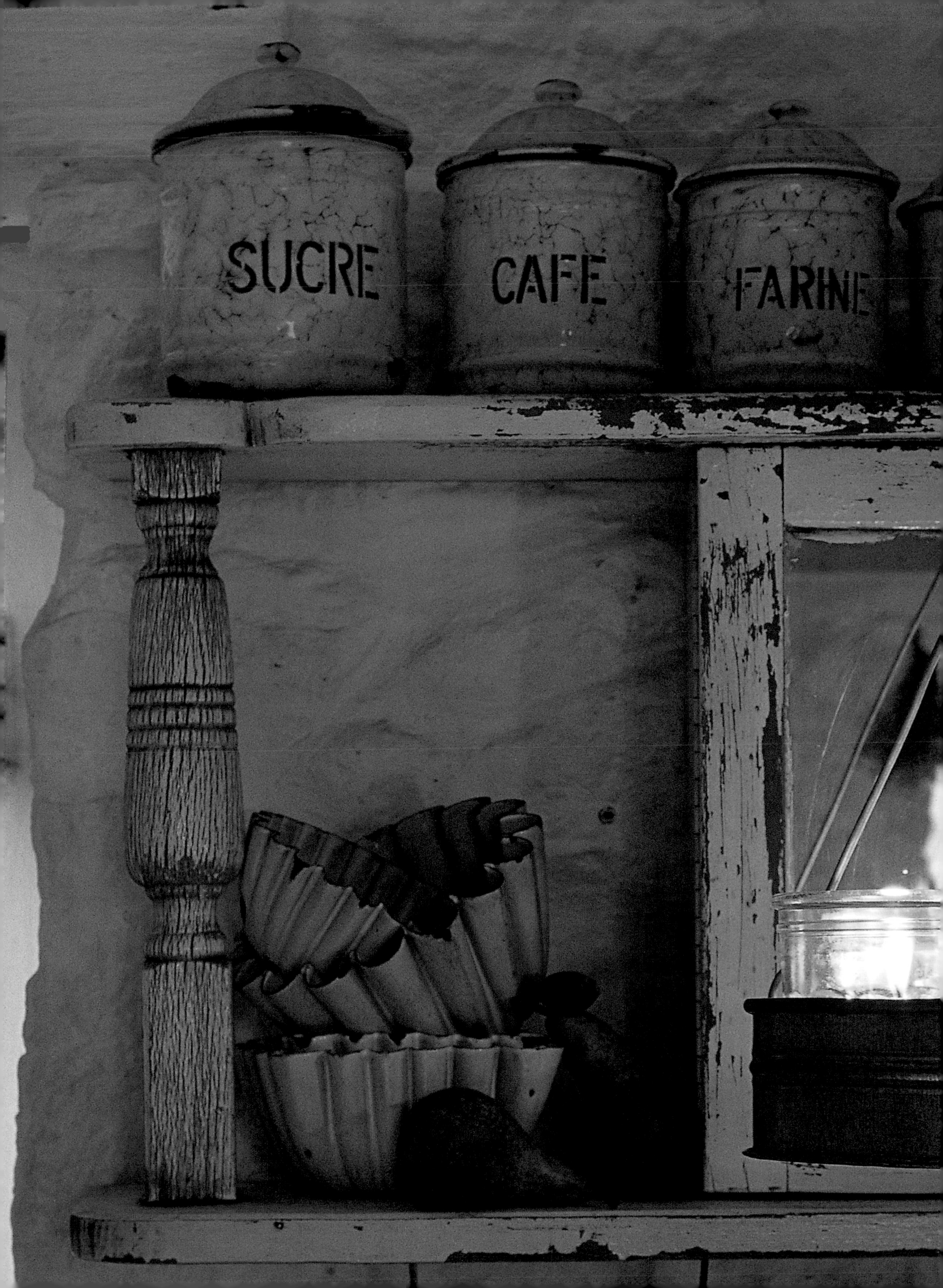
SUCRE
CAFE
FARINE

THROUGH THE HOME

E very single room in a house or apartment can benefit from the magic that candle flames bring. Lighting a candle is a simple way to bring instant atmosphere to the surroundings. One of the attractions of candles is that you can change the way you use them to create different styles and themes. In particular, use them to create elegant displays, highlighting features in a room.

Opposite: *A galvanized tray suspended from a kitchen ceiling becomes a glowing chandelier when filled with nightlights inside ordinary, everyday jam jars. The glass jars intensify the illumination from the flames.*

Above: *The fashionable appeal of galvanized metal home accessories encompasses candleholders as well.*

DECORATING WITH CANDLES

With their infinite versatility, candles can add their special qualities to both formal and informal surroundings, fitting easily into cosy sitting rooms, ordered dining rooms or rustic kitchens alike. By simply placing a candelabra on a dining table, or arranging a group of candlesticks on a coffee table, you can instantly transform a setting. Decorating with candles is creative and stimulating and the vast selection of candle accessories now available provides an inspiring starting point.

Candles should not be reserved just for special occasions – there is no reason why beauty and elegance should not be enjoyed on a daily basis. However, it is worth considering where they can be placed in a room to best effect. For example, candlesticks used to decorate a hall table or console table are more likely to serve an ornamental purpose and rarely be lit, except perhaps at times when you are entertaining on a grand scale. Candles that will be lit regularly should be placed in such a way that they make a focal point in the room, and where you can make the most of the light they give. It is also always advisable to place candles out of the way of draughts as they cause the candles to burn unevenly and to drip.

DINING ROOMS

Dining tables provide a perfect setting for candle arrangements such as centrepieces for both formal and informal occasions. A low central arrangement of candles, perhaps including fresh flowers, or candlesticks arranged in a symmetrical way to fit in a line along the centre of the table, will capture the gaze of all those present but not get in the way, so conversation can continue naturally around them. If a lack of space means a centrepiece is out of the question, then individual candles by each place setting provides a personal approach and simple solution.

KITCHENS

Kitchens pose practical considerations regarding where candles should be positioned. In a busy kitchen, a

Above: Candles bring a charm of their own to even the most informal kitchen table. A fruit basket with three integral candleholders and a simple black candelabra complement this rustic style with an unmistakable French influence.

Above right: An inexpensive metal chandelier made in Sweden might look as though it has been made out of wire coathangers but it brings a real sense of style to the corner of a sitting room. Moroccan tin lanterns and a Peruvian tin candlestick confirm that folk art treasures can be found all around the globe.

Opposite: An inviting table setting juxtaposes contemporary earthenware with traditional terracotta pots from the garden, for a look of understated chic. A group of small weathered pots, with glowing candle flames inside them, lights up a platter scattered with quail's eggs — a strikingly unusual way to serve the hors-d'oeuvre!

wire fruit bowl with candleholders incorporated into its shape will make a useful table centrepiece, with the varieties and colours of the replenished fruits providing an ever-changing effect. This type of container provides a good steady base for candles, so there is less danger of them being knocked over. Kitchens are often the hub of home life – and a chandelier over the table, where people tend to congregate, adds a dramatic flourish to the room, even when the candles are not alight. Using chandeliers can have practical benefits as well as exceptionally decorative ones. They are a good way of keeping candles out of the reach of children's hands. No one has to live in a house without candles just because they have a young family.

Kitchen tables are usually in constant use, and it can be annoying if you repeatedly have to move groups of candles out of the way to create more space. This problem can be solved by arranging candles displayed together on trays and platters that can be easily lifted out of the way to another part of the kitchen.

BATHROOMS

When choosing a decorating scheme for a bathroom, including candles might not immediately be a consideration, but they have a very special part to play in this room, as they do in every other part of the house. The best bathrooms provide a haven of retreat, a place where hopefully some moments of privacy may be enjoyed and an area in which people can relax and become rejuvenated. Candles are an important ingredient in helping to create this kind of atmosphere.

The main problem when using candles in a bathroom is usually where to put them. This room is often the smallest in the house and so it may not have much space for non-essential decoration. Lanterns and chandeliers offer an excellent solution because they do not encroach on valuable surface areas, and they can also look both exotic and flamboyant. Similarly, a small bracket shelf, tucked in a corner, will provide just enough room to take a lantern or single candlestick. Wall sconces also come into their own in a bathroom where space is at a premium.

Another way to brighten a bathroom is to decorate an empty windowsill with candles and holders embellished with shells, bringing a seaside theme into this room where water plays such an important part! Or you could display novelty-shaped soaps alongside moulded candles in similar shapes, such as fruits and shells. Candles can be bought that are moulded in the shape of Marseille soaps. Try using these placed beside the real thing for an original and humorous touch.

No matter which room in the house you choose to display your candles, they can only really be fully appreciated if a few basic safety principles are adhered to. The danger of the naked flame must never be underestimated. Never leave a burning flame unattended and keep naked

flames well away from furnishings and other flammable materials. Extinguish flames before they have burnt down to their candleholders – especially if they are surrounded by dried flowers or other materials which could easily catch alight.

Left: *One of the most restful pleasures in life is bathing by candlelight. The warm glowing flames create a sensuous, relaxing atmosphere which helps the stresses and strains of everyday living float away. A candle chandelier suspended over the bath would be the ultimate hedonistic treat.*

Opposite: *Even a rustic bathroom can benefit from the magic of candlelight. Here, miniature porcelain jelly moulds are used as tiny candleholders and the creamware candlesticks and an enamel candleholder complement this style.*

Above: *This rose-encrusted hand basin looks quite extraordinary, illuminated by a candelabra which includes a soap dish as part of the design. Not only does the basin have a wonderful floral border, but roses form the candleholders on the sconce and the hot and cold taps as well.*

STORING CANDLES

If you light the candles in your home regularly, you will need to keep a constant stock of them, to replenish those that are spent. Using bundles of candles as a decorative device is an excellent way of putting them to work and solves the problem of where to store them. A simple bundle can be used to decorate a shady windowsill or side table but always keep them out of the sun or warm places. Tie the bundles in different ways to suit a style, with shimmering taffeta ribbon, a cord with tassels or plain garden twine for a more down-to-earth approach. Alternatively, you can buy attractive metal or wooden storage boxes to hang on the wall. A basket filled with candles and placed on the floor is another decorative idea that you might like to consider.

Right: *Bundles of cream candles tied up with pretty ribbons have a similar look to laundered sheets and napkins in a linen cupboard. Obviously you should not store candles in a heated airing cupboard or they will end up softened and misshapen.*

FIREPLACES

Fireplaces are often a natural focal point in a room, with the furniture arranged facing or pointing towards them. The mantelpiece makes an excellent area to decorate with candles and their effect will not go to waste. The narrow ledge of space that a mantelpiece provides does restrict the holders you can use but still offers ample opportunities for lavish displays.

Symmetrically arranged candlesticks give a perfect sense of order and formality to a setting, so matching pairs work well, arranged on either side. In the same way, several sets of candlestick pairs can be placed in identical groups, using their variations in height to give an added interest. Candelabra that hold candles in a straight line bring an even more lavish effect. Candle shades, which

are available in patterns and colours to suit any decorative style, can be used to great advantage here.

Above the fireplace is an ideal place to use wall sconces. Again, a symmetrical arrangement of matching pairs always works well. Sconces that hold two or three candles increase the effect and give plenty of illumination when lit, resulting in a dazzling display. Alternatively, single candle sconces can be used just as effectively for a simpler look. They often incorporate reflective metal or mirrored plates behind the candle, as part of the design, to help to intensify the candlelight as well as adding another decorative feature. You can also buy wall sconces which include a bracket at the back, on which you can sit a favourite china dish behind the candle, and this will show off its ornamental qualities.

With space restricted, you do have to make sure that the candle flames are clear of the wall behind, for safety's sake. Always keep a watchful eye on candles when the fire is lit. They should never be in the line of direct heat because if the wax gets too warm, they may soften.

DRESSERS

Dressers make impressive display areas and are often laden with pretty china and decorative ceramics. Using candlesticks as part of this display is an opportunity to add another feature to a collection. Matching pieces, or items in a similar pattern, can be arranged in among the assorted bowls and platters. Many companies

that manufacture ceramic tableware and fine bone china include designs for candlesticks and holders as part of their ranges. Always make sure that candles are not placed directly underneath an overhanging shelf. A candle flame gives off a surprising amount of heat, which could damage or even set alight the shelf above if it is too close. Keep candles to the front of

shelves unless you plan to leave them unlit, as pure display.

Shallow nightlight holders again come into their own on dressers, and are a simple way of adding an extra decorative flourish to your furniture. Cabinets with a more formal design can be used to display candelabra and candlesticks, in the same way, combining fine china with any pieces of period silver you may be lucky enough to own.

Opposite far left: Rosy red apples, real and ornamental, add their natural charm to a colourful enamel stove and mantel shelf. Fruit-shaped candles look and smell so like the real thing that it is almost tempting to take a bite.

Opposite above: An old fireside range makes the focal point of the room and provides an ideal place to show off a collection of shiny tinware candelabra. Time has improved them with a worn and weathered look. An ornate tin mirror placed above them on the wall intensifies their shimmering light.

Opposite below: Brightly painted contemporary ceramics can be used to fill your home with colour and a range of patterns. Here, the work of potter Mary Rose Young includes a selection of candlesticks which match the china. Displayed on a dresser it makes a dazzling focal point.

Right: Turned wooden candlesticks, with painted and natural finishes, fit wonderfully into an English country setting, even though they often are actually made in India. Imported ethnic designs are worth looking out for and often incorporate distressed paint finishes which give the impression that the candlesticks have stood the test of time.

THEMES

The immense creative potential for using and displaying candles in the home often goes unrealized. Candles and candleholders come in so many shapes and sizes that they are an ideal way of enhancing a decorating theme and they can be chosen to suit any particular style, whether it be classical, simple, rustic or ethnic. So many items can be turned into innovative candleholders that once you start thinking of the possibilities you will realize the options for decorating with candles are endless.

Opposite: *For a table centrepiece at an outdoor party, decorate candles by tying vegetable leaves around them.*

Above: *An old silver candelabra takes on an elegant beauty when further embellished with twining ivy, white lilies and a single tulip.*

ENCHANTMENT BY CANDLELIGHT

G lass has a natural reflective quality that captures and radiates the glow of candlelight, intensifying its warm light. Even glass containers with nightlights inside them make shimmering displays. Also, cheap embossed pressed glass and old jam jars with relief patterns on them make excellent containers for candles because their delicate pat-terning is accentuated as the light shines through them. Pressed glass candlesticks and dishes can still be found in junk shops and a collection of these individual pieces looks most appealing when displayed together.

When candlesticks are arranged in a group, along with bowls, dishes and plates, it helps to build up impact and increase the illumination. You might even like to try using a pedestal cake stand to make a tiered tower with a candle placed at the centre on top. You can decorate each layer with candles and fresh flowers, always making sure that the glass or china layer above is clear of the flames below. Small dishes, ashtrays and salt cellars can also be transformed into simple candleholders.

Opposite: *Victorian pressed glass is still reasonably priced so a collection of pieces should not cost the earth. When used en masse and illuminated by candlelight, you can produce an effect with pressed glass arrangements that looks as though it must have cost much more than it did in reality. Stand plates on end behind the candlesticks and dishes, too, to make the most of any faceted patterns and intensify the effect.*

Right: *These gold-rimmed tumblers decorated with delicate patterns, simple bands and lattice designs are filled with scented candles. Displaying two or three together on a gilt-edged mirror makes the effect more dramatic and doubles the light they produce.*

Below: *Inexpensive embossed tumblers and old jam pots come alive when night-lights are lit inside each one. Here, a silver tray beneath them adds to the sparkle.*

SIMPLE PURITY

For a look imbued with simple purity, follow an all-white or cream colour theme. This approach fits into any setting and has a freshness and clarity with universal appeal. Creamware candlesticks used with pale beeswax candles provide the starting point to establish the style, and a group of these alone, displayed on surfaces covered with linen and lace, will instantly produce a stunning effect. White flowers, with a trace of green or the faintest pink blush can be added to include a suggestion of colour.

Creamware candlesticks and tableware have been made in England since the middle of the eighteenth century, and so they automatically generate a period feel with an enduring appeal and elegance. Candlesticks in the shapes of classical columns need only simple cream candles to show them off to their best. Pretty creamware plates, decorated with their distinctive pierced patterns, also make exquisite candleholders. Original creamware pieces are highly collectable but the designs are still being produced today.

Plaster mouldings and rosettes, intended for use as surface ornamentation on ceilings and walls, can be incorporated into displays to add an unusual architectural element. Their ornate relief patterns work wonderfully when combined with embossed and twisted candles. A traditional round ceiling rose can be turned into a large platter on which to stand lots of candles for a stunning table centrepiece. When the candles are alight, their amber glow will add warmth to the scene and pick up the patterns on the mouldings.

Opposite: *The beautiful relief patterns of feathers and scrolls on these plaster mouldings capture the light when the candles are lit. Try arranging embossed and plain pillar candles alongside the mouldings to show them at their best. Fragments of mouldings can be used in the same way, adding them to the display to produce a similar result.*

Above: *The thick pillar candles shown here incorporate a novel decorative device that also serves a practical purpose – the gold numeral, embossed on each candle, indicates the length of its burning time.*

Right: *A cream ceramic candleholder for two candles perfectly illustrates the essence of simple purity when arranged with a few blooms of white ranunculus. This uncomplicated display would look good in any setting.*

GOTHIC SPLENDOUR

Conjuring up the ambience of turreted castles and medieval splendour, Gothic style is bold and theatrical. Candles, chandeliers and floor-standing candelabra were an important part of this look in the sixteenth century, so using them to create the illusion of the period is an essential element. It is just a matter of scaling everything down to manageable proportions to suit your own home. Heraldic motifs such as fleurs-de-lys and crowns are integral to the theme, as well as ecclesiastically influenced designs – they are often used as decoration on candlesticks and wall sconces. A chandelier, hung from the ceiling by chains, or an ornate floor-standing candlestick or candelabra with tripod feet will instantly capture the spirit of the time and provide a strong focal point.

Brass, bronze, iron and wooden accessories complement each other when arranged together. Turned wooden bowls and heavy glass goblets are other decorative devices you might employ to strengthen the design. Stores which sell imported goods from the Far East are good places to start your search for dark wooden carved objects which capture the same mood. Church and beeswax candles are an obvious choice to incorporate in a Gothic display, but look out as well for other, more ornate candles which have the right feel and will add a finishing touch to your creation.

Right: *An iron fleur-de-lys wall sconce has a weathered look which suits the style and is in keeping with the lantern. Roughly cut-out shapes form a pattern in the metal to let the candlelight pass through. A green glass bowl sits comfortably in a black metal stand and is designed to hold a small candle.*

Above: *Brass candleholders with attractive filigree openwork decoration combine delicate patterning with a chunky feel – they need substantial pillar candles to balance their proportions. Unusual latticed candles add a colourful highlight and fit into the theme remarkably well. A simple brass candlestick with a fleur-de-lys stem completes the picture.*

Right: *A pewter pair of arms for a candelabra will convert an ordinary empty wine bottle into a splendid candleholder. A couple of crimson candles, decorated with gold motifs and tied with a shimmering filigree ribbon, and two crown votive candleholders have been used to reinforce the heraldic link. It is also worth looking out for gold and bejewelled candles with embossed designs – their ornate appearance will fit in well with this type of theme.*

CLASSICAL GRANDEUR

Decorating in a grand classical style is generally thought to be attainable only by the very wealthy, as its essence lies in the use of beautiful period furnishings and fine *objets d'art*. However, you can re-create the style in a much humbler fashion, without spending a fortune, by using some of the essential elements of the look and by interpreting them in a feasible way.

Candles bring their own magnificence to a scene, so with very little effort they can provide a starting point. It is then just a matter of incorporating appropriate decorative accessories to create a look that is truly inspirational. Silver-plated candelabra are made in reproduction designs of period styles. The brash shiny quality that reveals their origin soon mellows and softens to a more

desirable finish, so long as it is allowed to weather naturally. Display them with other pieces, such as platters, bowls and oval trays, and do not polish them too frequently. Ornate candlesticks and classic-shaped candelabra require only basic candles to illuminate them. For a feel of classic simplicity, it is hard to improve on cream, white and bleached beeswax candles.

Opposite: *A grand candlestick, with feather and scroll decoration, takes centre stage with a five-branched candelabra beside it. The top of the candelabra has an unusual stem, placed on top of an old decanter. The collection of glassware arranged around them combines fine examples and much humbler pieces but they all work well together. Collecting mismatched glassware means that you can build up a collection gradually.*

Above: *A butler's tray supports an extraordinary collection of paraphernalia, which includes an assortment of delicate glass funnels. The swirling candelabra with swooping arms is in fact only silver-plated and has benefited from being left to tarnish.*

Right: *A bundle of cream candles, tied together with a length of old gold braid, makes an elegant ornament.*

FLORAL ARRANGEMENTS

Candles can be included in flower arrangements to add another dimension to the design, incorporating their own ornamental and decorative qualities in among the plant materials. When the candles are lit, they will also bring out dazzling highlights, drawing attention to individual flowers and leaves. You might want to use candles in an arrangement for a particularly special occasion, to add an extra element to a floral centrepiece for an evening dinner table or, as part of a larger scheme, to decorate a mantelpiece. The mechanics needed to put it all together are surprisingly straightforward and once you know how it is done you will be amazed at the professional results you will be able to achieve. A good florist will be able to supply all the specialist materials that you will need.

A FLORAL MANTELPIECE

To decorate a whole mantelpiece, the lines of the arrangement need to be varied so that the height of the plant material is higher in some areas and lower in others to draw in the eye and create some interest. Putting an art nouveau bust at the centrepiece of this design creates a really distinct period feel which goes well with the iron fireplace. Thick ivory church candles are bold and classical enough to balance a strong centrally placed

ornament of this kind and prevent it from becoming too overpowering.

To decorate the mantelpiece, place blocks of wet florist's foam into enough florist's trays to cover its whole length. Secure the foam with florist's tape and put the trays in position. Then push the candles firmly down into the foam near the centre of the mantelpiece, arranging them in groups of varying heights. It is important that the candles are very stable and a good method of securing them is to attach three short lengths of wooden skewer or three stub (floral)

wires around the base of the candle with florist's tape and push these into the foam.

Next, push stems of ivy into the foam around the base of the candles to hide the foam. Add hydrangea stems, or the flowers of your choice, pushing them into the foam until it is completely covered. Keep looking at the arrangement from a distance as you work to check that it is taking shape in pleasing proportions. Finally, add focal flowers and interesting foliage in clusters, perhaps with roses as a finishing touch.

IVY CANDELABRA

A candelabra can be decorated with ivy and fresh flowers. Ivy is easy to find and makes an ideal base when wrapped around the arms of a candelabra. It needs only the simplest extra decorative touch, like displaying it in front of a mirror to give an exceptional result (see page 19).

Twine the ivy around the arms of the candelabra attaching it with florist's wire. Fix flowers in position in the same way, attaching them by twisting the wires over their stems and around the candelabra. Adding blackberries will create a contrast if you are using white flowers.

TABLE CENTREPIECE

You can make a stunning table centrepiece using a container meant especially for this purpose, or alternatively you can adapt something that you already have in your home such as a large fruitbowl, pedestal dish or cake stand. Remember to keep the container topped up with water and use a fine water spray to refresh the arrangement regularly.

Right: *An arrangement made in a ceramic pedestal dish makes a pleasing low focal point to decorate a table setting for a dinner party. The guests will be able to enjoy the stunning display but still be able to see each other above the candles during dinner conversation.*

Opposite: *Coloured pillar candles or even exotically shaped candles such as feathers could be used instead if you wish to achieve a different effect but, as flowers have such a natural beauty, it is often best to keep the candles simple. It does not matter if you have no statue – just work with whatever you have and think about which features of the fireplace you want to embellish before you begin. A smaller pale-coloured fire surround might suggest a lighter treatment, but the mechanics will be the same.*

First fill the container with wet florist's foam to make a good firm base to hold all your flowers and foliage. You will probably have to cut the foam to make it fit – it should stand above the level of the rim. Then push three candles of varying heights into the foam. Start to make the outline shape of the arrangement with stems of ivy and eucalyptus, until the foam is no longer visible.

Once this is complete, you can add the focal flowers. If you use soft-stemmed varieties like parrot tulips you may have to make holes in the foam with a knitting needle or twig. Position flowers in groups around the arrangement rather than dotting them throughout the shape. If the finished result is going to be seen from all sides, turn the container as you work.

CELESTIAL

S tars, suns and moons are popular decorative motifs which nev-
er fail to fascinate and attract. It is no
wonder that they have always held
such a strong allure – after all, they
are always in our view and in the
right weather they throw out their
own dazzling light. You can use candles to embellish a celestial theme
using gold as the predominant colour
and relying on these heavenly sym-
bols to add their own impact.

Candlelight looks wonderful when
reflected and radiating from gold surfaces; it gives a shimmering warmth
all around. Look out for brass lanterns and gilded wood and metal
candle accessories. Star-shaped candleholders and candlesticks are fairly
easy to find to establish the basis for
this style. If you happen to have any
gilded angels and cherubs, perhaps
packed away after Christmas, you can
add them to a display for an extra
divine flourish!

Right: *To add a decorative touch to a
plain candle, an embossed pattern has
been applied to an ivory church candle
using gold sealing wax. When the sealing
wax is alight, it is simply a matter of
allowing the drips to fall onto the candle
to make a pattern. You will need to
practise before you apply the pattern to
your candle. Another idea is to tie a piece
of gimp braid around the candle and apply
a blob of sealing wax over the knot,
pressing a fancy seal of a sun, moon or
star into the molten wax in keeping with
the celestial mood of the display.*

Right: *Halved coconut shells coated inside with a shimmering layer of gold leaf produce glimmering wells of light when the candles they contain are lit. Gold leaf is expensive but has a delicate papery quality that cannot be matched by using paint alone. The candle flames illuminate this textured lining to superb effect.*

Below: *Stars, moons and the odd cherub create a heavenly scene with universal appeal. Star candlesticks, holders and other star-patterned accessories are sold in numerous stores – in fact, this classic motif has been used as a decorative design for centuries. Beeswax candles add their natural golden colouring to the picture. However, ivory wax would blend just as well into the theme as a perfectly suitable alternative.*

COUNTRY STYLE

Candles fit perfectly into a simple country setting evoking the days when candles were the only light source after the daylight faded at sunset. Beekeeping is still mainly a country pursuit, and candle making used to be one of the apiarist's essential skills. The beeswax that remains after honey is removed from a comb was discovered to be far too valuable to go to waste. For centuries, beekeepers and candle makers have used the wax to make fragrant and slow-burning candles in natural shades. Candles in the shape of old-fashioned coiled beehives capture a rustic style instantly.

For candlesticks with a country feel the patina of age is a desirable finish; either cleverly mimic a worn and weathered look or find authentic examples. Turned wooden and painted candlesticks with the odd chip or

bash to add to the distressed finish, all help to add to the country feel. Enamel candleholders, 'Wee Willie Winkie' style, were once used to light the way to bed (the saucer at the base safely caught any dripping wax). If you manage to find any in junk shops, put them on display for a touch of genuine country charm. Choose rustic candelabra and chandeliers to complete the look.

Left: An old enamel candleholder may have a slightly chipped appearance but is still a very pretty way to support a candle. A faded green candle has been chosen to complement the delicate pink colour of the enamel.

Opposite: A verdigris-coloured finish on newly bought metal candlesticks mimics an effect that would take ages to occur naturally, instantly creating an ambience of homely informality. Their colour is set off well by the warm tones of rolled and moulded beeswax candles.

Left: Tinware candlesticks and lanterns possess a straightforward folk-art charm that suits a country setting. Shaker-style tinware candlesticks, punched tin lanterns and spill boxes were originally made from whatever basic materials were to hand, without any extra adornment to clutter the simple lines. They are still made today and the simplicity of this uncomplicated style remains both effective and appealing.

PROVENÇAL

Provence, in southern France, is an area steeped in tradition and colour – it makes a delightful theme to use to decorate your home. The region conjures up many images, especially fields of lavender and olive groves. It is also known for its brightly coloured fabrics printed with traditional designs taken from wooden blocks. They were first used in the eighteenth century and used to be printed by hand. Vivid ochre-glazed earthenware is another typical decorative speciality of the region. Candles can be easily incorporated into this style and will help to create a feel for the place or alternatively re-mind you of time spent there.

LAVENDER COLLARS

Provence is renowned for its laven-der and in the summer vast aromatic fields of these purple bushes domin-ate the landscape. You can use it to make pretty collars to decorate the base of your candles and lend its unmistakable fragrance to the room. Before you start, the lavender flow-ers and stems should be dry. They will need careful handling, because the brittle flowers can easily fall apart and become damaged. As you work the wonderful scent of the plant will permeate the air.

Make about 14 small bunches of lavender and hold the stems together with a few twists of fine florist's

wire. Cut the stems to the same length with florist's scissors. Bend a length of wire into a ring that fits comfortably around the base of the candle and will also sit on top of the candlestick. Wind several more thicknesses of wire round the ring, then loosely bind it all together by passing the wire all the way round the ring, cutting off any length of excess wire neatly.

Begin to lay the bunches one by one around the ring, keeping them pointing in the same direction all the way round. Fix each bunch in place by winding wire around both the ring and the stems. Make more bunches if necessary to complete the collar and cut the wire off neatly when the ring is completely covered. Thread a length of ribbon through a gap between the wires underneath and tie into a bow with trailing ends.

Opposite: *Aromatic lavender collars with ribbon bows decorate barley-twist candles in pale natural wooden candlesticks for a taste of Provence. Do not let the flames burn down to the level of the dried lavender. The moulded candles in the shape of lavender bundles in the background are made from scented wax which perfumes the air as they burn.*

Right: *Traditional faience earthenware with its rich ochre glazes is a typical feature of Provence. Here, miniature ceramic urns have been used to make garden candles, reflecting the classic lines of traditional garden urns. The wax contains an insect repellant to ward off unwelcome mosquitoes and midges on summer evenings.*

FIRE AND WATER

Water is one of the most romantic ways of displaying and presenting candles; the dancing light of the flame reflects in the water and creates a beautiful hypnotic effect. Candles can be floated in all kinds of containers; coloured and frosted glass adds another reflective dimension. The addition of fresh flowerheads on the surface of the water, and coloured glass nuggets or marbles in the bottom of the bowl, help to create entrancing combinations of colour and scent. Always make sure that the flowers you choose to float among the candles are not too heavy. They should be as flat as possible with a symmetrical shape that will bob on the surface of the water in a balanced way.

Individual drinking glasses, goblets and water glasses can also be used as containers to float candles. These can be placed by each place setting at the dinner table. Keep the water level near to the rim of the glass so that there is no danger of the flame causing it to crack. Similarly, earthenware fruit bowls and enamel basins will provide different types of container for floating candles.

Flower-shaped floating candles come in a vast range of colours as do other shapes like hearts, stars and plain round disks. Today, seaside related shapes such as shells, starfish and boats are also popular.

Opposite and above: *These floating flower candles in a glass bowl have individual hydrangea petals and leaves scattered in among them in similar pastel shades. Glass nuggets lining the base of the bowl make a transparent coloured background beneath the flowers. Glass bowls with textured, faceted and embossed surfaces as well as shiny metal kinds make the most of floating candles, adding to the sparkling effect when the candles are lit.*

Left: *This cone-shaped glass container sitting on a metal frame is specially made to hold a floating candle. Adding an orange ranunculus and an apricot pansy head beside the candle makes a simple but sumptuous decoration.*

OUTDOOR FLAMES

Decorating the garden with candles for an outdoor party is an enjoyable way to make the event especially memorable. Pathways and patios can be lined with candles placed in jars or small paper bags filled with sand, and groups of lanterns can be used to highlight focal points such as a pond or a statue. Alternatively, you can take the garden theme and use it to bring your vegetable patch inside your home.

Terracotta pots make ideal containers for candles and are so complete in themselves that no other embellishment is needed. The older, more aged and weathered they become, the better they seem to look. If you have new pots which are rather pristine, they can be made more stylish by painting the insides gold. When the candles burn down the flames will reflect off the gold, creating a wonderful glow. Rather than placing a candle in a pot, you can buy candles which are made in flower pots.

Opposite: *A potting shed makes the perfect setting for a colourful crop of vegetable candles. Bundles of carrots, maize and asparagus look good enough to eat, tied together with strands of raffia, and make novel shapes for moulded candles. A miniature cauliflower looks splendid in its peat pot with pumpkin and gourd candles taking the theme further. You could always decorate a dresser in your kitchen with this type of candle and display a basket of real vegetables beside them for a visual feast.*

Opposite: *A fine collection of weathered old terracotta pots in a shady corner of the garden takes on a dramatic look when they are filled* en masse *with candles. To use this decorative idea, be bold and arrange the pots in large quantities. Here, ivy and other seedlings growing naturally in among them add the only extra ornamentation, with an old tin watering can, which has stood the test of time, completing this horticultural delight.*

For a table centrepiece, fill a trug or shallow basket with vegetables and wedge vegetable-shaped candles in between, perhaps with pebbles helping to hold them firmly upright. For a garden party, you could decorate plain candles in a fun way to

Right: *Tiny glass lanterns with wire handles bring a colourful sparkle to a small tree in the garden and look like pretty fairy lights. They are just large enough to hold a nightlight which will provide a colourful glow when lit. Wire handles make it easy to suspend them safely from the branches.*

follow the garden theme, by tying bunches of radish, curly cabbage leaves and runner beans around simple pillar candles. Use several strands of coloured raffia together to wrap around them and tie with a flourish into a bow. The outer spiky casing that surrounds a horse chestnut makes an effective and amusing small candleholder.

SEASONS

I n the same way that flora and fauna change in an annual cycle – with the colours of flowers and plants often indicating the time of year – candles can be used as part of sumptuous displays to celebrate the passing of the seasons. You can either buy moulded candles in the shapes of flowers and leaves which instantly conjure up the atmosphere of the season, or there are many simple ideas for decorative touches which you can make yourself to reflect the time of year.

Opposite: *Shop-bought leaf-and flower-shaped candles can look extremely lifelike and instantly capture the atmosphere of summer days in the garden.*

Above: *Adding a plume of leaves in subtle autumn shades to the base of a candle in a similar tone is an easy way to add a seasonal touch to a candle.*

SPRING

I n the season of rejuvenation and new beginnings, spring flowers like delicate snowdrops, narcissi and primroses provide a pastel palette of colours that can be combined beautifully with candles. There is always a feeling of optimism and excitement as the garden comes to life and begins again its natural yearly cycle. Bare wood that has lain dormant for several months never ceases to amaze as fluffy buds emerge and catkins and pussy willow clothe the branches. In spring, the days start to lengthen but the evenings still draw in early enough to benefit from the magic of candlelight.

MOSSY POTS

Mossy pots make pretty containers for candles and are easy to make. You can find carpet moss on woodland walks or a good florist should be able to supply you with it. If possible, use old weathered terracotta plant pots or else buy plain pots which are large enough to hold a nightlight or a small pillar candle.

To make the candleholders, simply wrap pieces of carpet moss around the pots and tie them in place with garden twine.

Right: *Candles burning in mossy pots take on a natural beauty when arranged with woodland flowers and spring bulbs growing in weathered terracotta pots.*

Left: *To bring a feeling of spring into the home, you can combine the bareness of stone and earthenware with exotic blooms in fresh pale shades.*

Below: *Antique glass hyacinth holders are highly collectable and can be found in delicate colours and pretty fluted shapes. You can use them to make candleholders by pushing tightly compacted moss into their narrow necks. A candle pushed into the moss will then be held firmly in place. Treat other small vases and bowls in the same way and try to include glasses with hyacinths or amaryllis growing in them as part of the display. Do not allow the candles to burn down within a few centimetres of the moss. Under no circumstances leave a burning candle unattended.*

SUMMER

During the long days of summer, the garden and outdoor living dominate the lifestyles of many. The garden is permeated with fragrances and glorious flowers. Hopefully fine weather and warm sunny days mean that more time can be spent following outdoor pursuits. Candles and garden flares can be used to decorate the garden, making it possible to stay outside as daylight fades. Similarly trees can be lit with lanterns, and both candles and lanterns may be used to illuminate tables for alfresco dining.

Back in the house or apartment, doors and windows leading to a garden are more likely to be kept open. Using brightly coloured candles that echo the colours of flowers growing outside, as well as flower-shaped candles and candleholders, helps to bring the garden nearer. Baskets of flowers mingled with candles in an arrangement have a similar effect.

Using candlesticks with flower-shaped holders is an effective way of emphasizing a floral style, made possible during the summer months. At other times of year they will also evoke the pleasures of summertime and help to remind you of warm relaxing days spent lazily out in the open air.

Below: *Here a wire basket has an inner lining which can be filled with water and a mesh grid which holds plant stems steady. Decorative tulip candlesticks are part of the design, which is specifically made so that fresh flowers and candles may be arranged together, with the flames burning above the flowers and foliage.*

Opposite: *Novelty-shaped candles have shaken off their rather kitsch image and now come in remarkably realistic designs which capture the beauty of the real things they mimic. As well as floating daisy and anemone candles, baskets of blooms capture the feel and symmetry of a formal garden.*

AUTUMN

In the 'season of mists and mellow fruitfulness', subtle shades of russet, bronze, brown and gold gradually emerge in the countryside and garden as the summer foliage changes colour. Although the natural world is now beginning a period of winding down, it is a time of great vibrancy with a rich harvest of fruits and berries in plentiful supply, inspiring plenty of decorative ideas.

Berried foliage and gently dying leaves are perfect partners for candlelight and provide opportunities for decorating the house. Candles are available to complement all of these shades and lend a touch of warmth during the cold months ahead. Wonderful candles in shapes of autumn fruits and leaves can also be found.

AUTUMN LEAF PLUMES
A simple but very effective way to decorate candles in a candelabra is to tie bundles of autumn leaves to the base of each candle. Virginia creeper leaves take on a magnificent range of shades before they fall off the vines. Other leaves could be substituted, although larger leaves will obviously need to be placed around a bigger candle to keep the proportions balanced. Remember to extinguish the flames before they reach the level of the leaves.

Opposite: *This black metal candelabra has oak leaf shapes as part of its design and is exactly in keeping with the mood of the season. Home-made plumed candles will add an extra flourish.*

Select your leaves to give a varied spectrum of shades with the odd surprise of a paler tone included. Choose candles made from wax dyed in a colour that augments the colours of the leaves. You will find natural raffia twine at garden centres and in other dyed shades at craft shops.

Bunch the leaves together at the base of the candle, leaving enough space for the candle to fit into the candleholder. Hold them in place with one hand and wind strands of raffia around them to fix them in place. Tie the raffia with a knot, cut the ends and shred them as the finishing touch.

Left: *Wooden candleholders painted with autumnal fruit and vine designs complement a seasonal theme. Russet spray chrysanthemums, Michaelmas daisies, berried branches, autumn leaves and orchard fruits make a stunning display with vibrant contrasts.*

WINTER

During the cold, stark months of winter the garden lies dormant and the daylight hours are at their shortest. Now, especially, candles come into their own to lift everyone's spirits. As well as branches of colourful berries that can be used in winter candle displays, other elements can be drawn from the season to create a particular look. Shop-bought candles made to look like bare twigs match the bareness of the trees outside and can be put to good decorative use inside the house. Taking these as a starting point, it is possible to build on the theme to create a winter look with a rustic feel. Alternatively, choose frosted glass candlesticks and nightlight holders to echo an icy white blanket outside.

Opposite: Strips of bark, found on woodland walks, can be used to wrap around existing candles to give them a seasonal woody feel. When you wrap leaves or arrange twigs around the sides of glass nightlight holders, fix them with a length of garden twine.

Left: Elegant silver candleholders holding small candles balance along a natural ledge made by a woody vine. Shaped weights at the bottom of each long stem provide the equilibrium necessary to keep the candles upright.

Below: Frosted glass candleholders link their icy whiteness with the warm glow of candle flames. Frosted glass tumblers work just as well if they are lit by nightlights.

SPECIAL OCCASIONS

Throughout the year our lives are plotted around significant occasions marked on the calendar to celebrate events, traditions and rituals, Candlelight adds a touch of magic to any special day and can help to turn it into a real celebration. An ever-increasing array of candles and candleholders is now available, designed to suit specific occasions and holidays. However, it is also easy to make original and innovative candles and accessories yourself.

Opposite: *This wonderful display of candles using delicate china as candleholders is perfect for a smart tea party. For a more relaxed occasion, use rustic pottery decorated with chunkier candles.*

Above: *An impressive Hallowe'en display of ornamental gourds.*

WEDDING

The romance of candlelight and weddings go hand in hand, especially if you use candles to decorate the tables for a reception or evening party. White is the normal colour for a wedding – and an easy colour scheme to follow. However, it is becoming more popular for a bride to choose another colour for her dress and this can be picked up in the flower and candle arrangements. Popular floral colours include classic white and creams with lilies and stephanotis, deep pastels and bright cottage garden flowers or even rich burgundy and russet shades for an autumn wedding. Candlesticks, holders, a chandelier or candelabra make excellent wedding presents, particularly if they are accompanied by a box of ivory candles perhaps tied with a band of cream lace.

Above: *Thick pillar candles will burn for hours, which is just what is required at a wedding party that will go on into the night. Here, white pillars with vertical ridges embossing the surfaces are simply placed on squares of marble, held firmly in place with tabs of candle fix. You could stencil batches of white or ivory pillar candles with silver or gold paint for a more ornate look.*

Left: *This group of Indian embossed candlesticks made of inexpensive matt (flat) silver aluminium shows how a variety of similar but different designs can look good together. There is no need for everything to match to produce a stunning look – basic white candles may be all that is needed. They are also available cheaply in large quantities, making them ideal for a party. Ribbon bows of silky braid have been tied around the stems for a delicate finishing touch.*

CHRISTENING

A christening or similar non-religious ceremony is a family celebration that allows everyone the opportunity to welcome a new person into the family and give the young child their official name. Candles often form part of the celebration but, as it is highly likely that children will be present, they need to be used sparingly and placed away from inquisitive tiny hands. This is a good opportunity for children to experience the magic that candlelight helps to create and also learn that candles are to be admired and not to be played with.

MOSSY BEAR CANDLEHOLDER

Animal-shaped candleholders provide a theme that is attractive to children and adults alike. They make a suitable centrepiece for the buffet table after a christening and would even make an inexpensive present. Other animal shapes, perhaps a rabbit or lamb, can be made in the same way as this bear. The method involves making a wire-mesh frame from chicken wire. You can always use a real teddy bear as a model if you are unsure about shape and proportions. There is no need to be too meticulous so long as the shape conveys the general idea – the moss will make the finished animal much chunkier, so keep this in mind. Use deep green carpet moss available from florists to cover the mesh frame.

HOW TO MAKE THE BEAR

Look for chicken wire with a fairly fine mesh so that it is easy to bend. It can be hard on your hands pulling and pushing the mesh into shape, so watch out for sharp scratchy ends while you work. Mould the head and torso from a rectangular piece of

chicken wire by bending it into a tube and joining the pointed ends of wire together by twisting. (Any sharp ends should always be pushed inside the frame.) To make the neck, gather the tube in by pulling the mesh together about a third of the way down its length. Join together both ends of the tube and then round each end off.

For the head, manipulate the mesh by pushing and pulling until a satisfactory shape is formed. Make the arms and legs separately and then join them to the bear by twisting the jagged wire-ended limbs around the mesh of the torso. At the end of one paw, push in the candle to give a firm base which will hold it steady.

Lay carpet moss on top of the chicken wire and fix it in position with short lengths of stub (floral) wire bent into U-shaped pins, until all the mesh is covered. Finally, tie a ribbon bow around the neck.

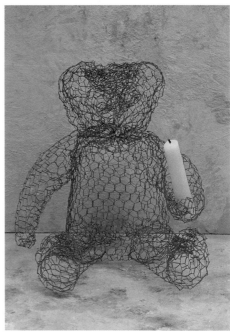

Above: *Animal-shaped candleholders provide a theme that is attractive to children and adults alike. Other animal shapes, perhaps a rabbit or lamb, can be made in the same way as this mossy bear.*

MOTHER'S DAY

In the United States of America, Mother's Day is the second Sunday in May, while in Britain Mothering Sunday is the fourth Sunday in Lent. Both were established as annual commemorations of mothers and motherhood. Mother's Day is an opportunity to make an effort to recognize the special role that mothers play. The giving of gifts and cards is the traditional way to do this.

Like many other occasions, the commercialization of the event sometimes seems to overshadow the real sentiments behind the tradition. Giving a present that you have made yourself and making decorations for a special Mother's Day get-together adds a personal touch that rekindles the original emotion behind it all. Most mothers will certainly appreciate a beautiful flower/candle gift.

An unusual way to display candles for Mother's Day is to use bone china cups and saucers. Crockery odd-ments found in junk shops are ideal, although you could be brave and use your best china! Any odd drips of wax that might form can easily be removed later by carefully lifting dried blobs from the surface of the porcelain first, then immersing the item in hot water.

DRYING PANSIES

Pansies have an irresistible charm with their cheery faces in beautiful subtle shades and velvety markings. The flowerheads are very easy to dry and use as candle decorations for a special Mother's Day gift.

Silica gel, a chemical drying medium, helps to give lifelike results when you dry flowers, enabling them to retain their colour and shape. Place the flowers in layers, separated by silica gel, inside an airtight container or a tin with a lid. Gently sprinkle spoonfuls of silica gel around the blooms, keeping the pet-als flat. The last layer of flowerheads needs to be completely covered with the gel before you secure the lid.

Pansies only take around 24 hours to dry – if left longer than this they

will become so brittle that they just crumble and will be impossible to work with. Remove the dried flowers from the gel and store them in an airtight box. Separate them with sheets of greaseproof (wax) paper and sprinkle them with a few more crystals of silica gel. Always keep them away from bright sunlight.

Use the dried flowerheads to decorate your candles. Melt a small amount of wax glue and apply it with a small brush to the backs of the petals, then press each flower in place. Once the candles are decorated, they need to be dipped once in a dipping can full of molten paraffin wax to give a protective coating.

Left: *Pillar candles in soft blue and lavender-coloured wax go particularly well with pansies.*

St Valentine's Day

Hearts are the traditional symbol of love frequently used to decorate cards, cakes and ornaments to celebrate St Valentine's Day and give to those we love. On this day, custom decrees that secret admirers anonymously send cards or tokens to their loved ones. Candles and candle-light all add to the romance of the occasion.

Heart candleholders

To make a heart candleholder, choose empty aluminium cans with attractively coloured surfaces. If the outsides are too dominant, you can paint them, or rub them lightly with sandpaper to dull them.

If you plan to make matching candleholders, it is best to work with a paper template. Wrap a piece of paper around a can and draw a scalloped line for the front edge of the holder. Cut out the template then wrap it around the can, secure with tape and draw around it in pencil. Cut along the outline. Use a dress-maker's tracing wheel to make pin-

prick marks to decorate the metal, following the outline of the shape and piercing it right through with a needle or bradawl (awl) in places. The scallops along the front edge can be bent down and a fringed tassel cut into the metal at the top to complete the candleholder.

Above: *Few people will realize that these candleholders have been created out of drinks (soda) cans.*

Left: *To create a romantic look for St Valentine's Day, choose candles in reds and deep pinks, scented with sensuous fragrances. Small shop-bought heart-shaped candles can be used as floating candles or placed on pretty china saucers and dishes. A heart-shaped wire basket makes a perfect shallow tray container to fill with small scented pillar candles, burning at different heights and embellished further with flowers. Glass-lined metal candleholders for nightlight candles reveal a heart-shaped glow through cut-out holes in the sides.*

CHRISTMAS

Christmas is the perfect time to go to town decorating your home. Alongside shelves of baubles and garlands, stores are packed with candles and candleholders in novelty festive colours and shapes, to decorate the home following any theme or to give as gifts.

CANDLES ON THE CHRISTMAS TREE

After looking up at a starry sky from beneath a wood of tall pines and witnessing the stars twinkling through the trees, Martin Luther, the sixteenth-century religious reformer, reputedly put the first candles on a tree to recreate the dazzling scene that he had witnessed. Since then, the use of tree candles has been greatly eclipsed by electric tree lights, which are a much safer way to illuminate a tree. Yet for some, the desire to capture that same magic that Martin Luther sought to achieve with real candles remains strong today.

Candleholders are often pretty decorations in their own right so it is not always necessary to light the candles to enjoy them. The holders either clip on to the tree's branches or are balanced by a weighted bead or medallion which holds them upright.

Lighting real candles on a tree is extremely hazardous and calls for great care. A cut tree kept indoors over several weeks dries out and becomes highly flammable, so always keep the tree in a container which holds water and keep it topped up throughout the festivities. Choose the positions of the candles carefully, with no overhanging branches or decorations in the way of the flames, and do not allow the candles to burn right down. For a safer alternative, tie small bundles of candles on to the trees branches to make tree decorations.

AN ADVENT RING

The countdown to Christmas is a large part of the excitement and fun of the impending celebrations, especially for children. The four weeks of Advent that precede Christmas are a time of activity and preparation – and marking each week as it passes is a wonderful way for the family to share the anticipation together. Children often have Advent calendars with one window to mark each day.

Candles have always formed a part of this ritual and a wonderful idea for adults is to make an Advent ring. Advent candles marked with 24 numbered divisions are lit and allowed to burn down one section daily until Christmas Eve. Another type of Advent ring is a decorative wreath of fresh foliage and fruits which holds four candles within its circle. On the first Sunday of Advent one candle is lit, on the second two are lit and so on until all four candles are ceremoniously lit together on the last Sunday. To keep the leaves looking fresh throughout the month, spray them with water from time to time and remember to extinguish the flames before they reach the leaves.

Opposite: *Painted candlesticks in red, green and cream make an impressive group combined with a verdigris candelabra to give quite a traditional look, but with contemporary freshness. The candles have been chosen in cream and soft greeny blue tones to complement the candleholders.*

Above: *A traditional Advent ring helps to mark the four weeks leading up to Christmas. Here it is shown surrounded by other seasonal produce like colourful fruits and aromatic spices which are associated with this time of year. Modern Christmas china with a sponged holly design includes candlesticks as part of the range. This adds further festive charm to the display.*

A wreath base made of florist's foam will make a good frame for an Advent ring. Use four ivory church candles for this wreath. Church candles have a high proportion of beeswax, so they will burn for a long time. The most appropriate foliage is branches of fir and berried ivy, with small cones and miniature rosy red apples arranged among it. The only other materials you will need are stub (floral) wires and scissors.

To make the wreath, push the candles into the foam ring to divide it into quarters and soak the base in water before pushing short stems of foliage into the foam. Work all around the ring until the foam is completely covered. Use short lengths of stub wire to pierce the fruits, twisting the ends together and leaving a long end to push into the foam. To wire the cones, wrap a length of stub wire around the base of each, twist the ends and leave a long end of wire as before. Arrange the fruit among the foliage, pushing the wires into the foam.

HALLOWE'EN

As Hallowe'en celebrations generally take place at night, candlelight forms an intrinsic part of the atmosphere. You can buy Hallowe'en candles in pumpkin shapes as well as novelty candles in traditional Hallowe'en motifs like witches and black cats. Traditionally, hollowed pumpkins are carved by children to make lanterns, with simple geometric shapes cut out to make ghoulish faces with jagged teeth that the candlelight will glow through.

Dark red swedes can be used in the same way, with their flesh gouged out and faces carved into the vegetable skin. They need a string handle attached if they are to be carried in a night-time procession. The rich colours of gourds and pumpkins – in warm yellow and amber with a ridged texture and interesting mottled markings – always make a dazzling seasonal display.

GOURD CANDLEHOLDERS
Ornamental gourds can be used to make unusual candleholders for a seasonal display. Plan a group of these candleholders, choosing various colours, textures, shapes and sizes. Make sure they will naturally sit steady and have a good solid base, then gouge out a hole in the top of each to take a candle snugly. Try to select candles in shades that will complement the different colours of the gourds.

LANTERNS
As well as faces, you can create other more unusual designs of swirling filigree lines, stars and leaf shapes which look spectacular when a candle's flame glows through them. To make them you will need a small sharp knife or, even better, a lino (linoleum knife) or woodcutting tool

which will easily carve V-shaped slices and cuts from the pumpkin.

Carve the patterns freehand on the skin or draw them lightly first with a pencil, biro, or a fibre-tipped pen if you are not too confident. As you make the design, think about where the top will be sliced off to make the lid of the lantern.

Remember that a candle needs air to be able to burn properly, so incorporate holes in the pattern which will provide an adequate air supply. Carve lines and shapes into the skin in ridges – about 5–10mm (¼–½in) deep, but you do not have to be too

Above: *Hollowed out pumpkins are the simplest, and yet most effective, Hallowe'en candleholders.*

precise. When the carving is complete, cut off the top with a straight, zigzag or scalloped edge, making a corresponding key on both the lid and the base so that you know which way the lid fits on. Scoop out the flesh from the inside of the pumpkin leaving the sides about 1cm (½in) thick or a little more, depending on the size of the pumpkin. You can use the unwanted flesh centre to make a sweet and spicy pumpkin pie.

BIRTHDAY

B lowing out the candles on a birthday cake and making a wish is part of traditional birthday celebrations and still holds a childish excitement even for adults. A birthday is often a child's first experience of the enjoyment and ceremony that candles can bring to a special occasion. The tradition goes that all the candles must be extinguished with one puff if the wish is to come true. It is also important not to share the wish with anyone or the spell may well be broken.

The candles on the cake – one for each year of the birthday boy or girl's life – can be bought in miniature twists and tapers in bright vibrant colours. Candles moulded in the shapes of numbers are also available today. Small candles are usually held in plastic candleholders with scalloped petal edges and a spiked base that pushes easily into icing (frosting). They come in different colours – mainly pastel shades, gold or silver.

FOIL CAKE FLOWERS

To decorate a chocolate birthday cake with an original flourish, try painting silver plastic candleholders with stained-glass paints which come in vibrant transparent colours. These produce a shimmering metallic range of colours when applied over silver plastic. Flower-shaped collars cut out of foil pudding basins can be given the same treatment to surround the candleholders. It is best to apply the paint only to the top side of the foil so that it does not come into contact with the cake.

Above: *This scrumptious chocolate cake is decorated with painted candleholders and flower surrounds, set off by brightly coloured twisted candles. Anyone would be thrilled to be presented with it as part of their birthday celebrations. Shop-bought flower candles are another unusual and alternative way to decorate a cake and also look pretty bunched in groups to make a bouquet.*

59

GARDEN PARTY

When the sun shines and the garden reaches its horticultural peak, filled with an abundance of colourful flowers and scented summer blooms, there is no better time to celebrate the visual delights of the season. Candles can be used to decorate a summer buffet table for a garden party and add to the sumptuousness of the occasion. They will also help to provide much-needed illumination for long evening suppers and barbecues as the sun fades and dusk sets in.

Fruit-shaped candles can be used to complement platters of the real thing. Candles are available in uncannily realistic forms of soft fruits, peaches and strawberries, as well as orchard fruits such as apples and pears. Blooms of floating flower can-

dles fit just as well into a garden setting. Use lanterns to help to keep candles alight in breezy weather – or colourful glass containers which will accentuate the colours of any nearby blossom. Glass lanterns can be hung to add glowing splashes of colour to the branches of surrounding trees or to highlight focal points.

Above: *A table in the garden laden with fruits of the season is colourful and attractive, with candles and containers illuminating the summer scene. Glass lanterns and candleholders provide some protection for flames, which will still dance in the breeze but have a better chance of staying alight. The green glass tumbler containers have a crazed finish of fine cracks which catch the light.*

Left: *Candles moulded into the shape of fruits can look almost indistinguishable from the real thing, particularly if they are scented with the relevant fruity perfume as well.*

EASTER

For centuries, eggs have been used as a symbolic motif in the folk art of many countries around the world. Traditionally, an egg is an emblem used to represent new life and the fresh beginnings that are celebrated by Christians at Easter as well as marking the arrival of spring.

Eggs have always fascinated designers and craftsmen and are frequently decorated – with designs ranging from the naive and colourfully simple approach of children to fantastically ornate and exquisitely bejewelled Fabergé eggs. Easter and eggs will always be special subjects for candle displays.

DUCK EGG CANDLES

Duck's eggs are slightly larger than hen's eggs and can sometimes be found with pretty powder-blue shells as well as in their more usual white. It you carefully break off the tops and remove the runny middles, you can use the empty shells to make pretty container candles.

Gently wash the shells to remove any albumen that remains inside and leave the shells to dry thoroughly before making the candles. Make sure that there are no cracks in the shells which might allow the wax to leak out of the shells. Melt paraffin wax in the top of a double boiler, then fill the eggs not quite to the top with the molten wax. When the wax is partly set and will hold a wick in place upright, push a length of container wick into the centre of each eggshell, then leave the wax to set. As the wax cools and a well forms, reheat the wax and top the eggs up with more wax. Trim the wick to 1cm (½in) and leave the candles to cool for at least an hour before lighting them.

Top: *Shop-bought candles are easy to display by using pretty china eggcups as candleholders. You can mix them with hand-painted hard-boiled eggs, for a colourful seasonal effect. Some of them look good enough to eat!*

Above: *Egg candles can be bought that look just like real free-range versions. They are easy to make yourself using egg-shaped moulds that split in half to release the candle when the wax has set. Plain white paraffin wax with some stearin added will produce lifelike results.*

CANDLE
MAKING

TYPES OF CANDLES

The art of candle making and the way in which candles are designed have come a long way since the days when candles were the only means for people to light their homes. Today, they are available in so many sizes, shapes and colours that it is almost impossible to imagine a candle that you would not be able to find, if you were determined to buy a specific type to fit into a colour scheme or decorative plan. But although you can buy numerous candles in a range of different shapes, colours and sizes, remember that, once you have learned the skills involved, it is also easy to make your own.

Opposite: *Wax can be dipped, moulded, rolled, contained or carved to make an endless variety of candles.*

Above: *Stained-glass candles.*

A GALLERY OF CANDLES

As a general rule, it is preferable to store candles in a horizontal position but they will not come to any harm if they are stood upright, packed tightly in a box. The most important requirement is that they should be out of direct sunlight so that there is no chance of them melting or of their colours fading. Candles can also be stored so that they become a decorative feature – pairs of dipped candles hanging on a wall can look very cheerful and effective.

DIPPED CANDLES

The most basic and traditional types of candle are those that are made by the dipping method. This is how candles have been produced for centuries. The process involves taking a wick and dipping it into a large can of molten wax. The wax is left to dry after each dip and the process is then repeated. Each time the wick is dipped into the wax, the shape of the candle is gradually built up and formed. The resulting candles may be slender and tapered, very long and elegant, or as short as you like, depending on the length of the wick.

Dipped candles are generally made in pairs, although it is possible to dip them singly. If candles are dipped in pairs, they are particularly easy to store by hanging them over a hook on a wall. When they are made commercially, the production lines include frames that dip several candles at once.

STRAIGHT-SIDED CANDLES

Most candles were made by the dipping method until stearin was developed in the early nineteenth century. This was found to be an excellent shrinking agent for wax which enabled candles to be moulded in pillar shapes and subsequently into other

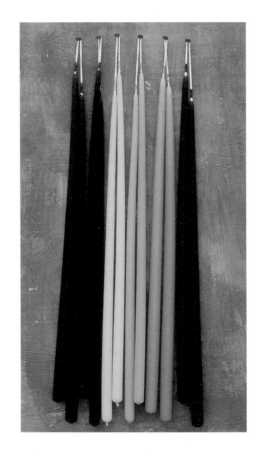

Above: *Dipped candles.*
Below: *Beeswax candles.*

designs as well. Stearin also helps to prevent candles from dripping. After stearin's properties had been discovered, the whole candle making process became much more refined and resulted in candles which were greatly improved in quality. As with dipped candles, straight-sided candles are available in an enormous range of colours. The majority are made to a standard size, which can be used in most candlesticks.

BEESWAX CANDLES

Beeswax has most unusual and fascinating qualities. Not only does it smell wonderful when it is burned but in its natural state beeswax is a beautiful honey colour which has a homely charm. Although it does cost more than paraffin wax, it is particularly useful because it lengthens the burning time of a candle.

The wax itself is a by-product of bee-keeping – indeed, candle making often used to go hand in hand with the apiarist's craft. Unlike paraffin

wax, beeswax has a very sticky quality when it is being worked which means that pure beeswax candles generally need to be dipped or rolled. Some beeswax candles can be moulded but a special release agent must be used on the inside of the mould (you can obtain this from candle-making suppliers) or it will be almost impossible to get the candle out of the mould when it has set.

As it is comparatively expensive, a little beeswax is often used simply to improve the quality of paraffin wax that is being used for making dipped or moulded candles – any amount may be added. Most frequently, beeswax is bought in sheets. These are mainly available in its natural colour but you can also buy sheets in green, red, white and bright blue, and in pastel variations on these. Today, you can even buy small beeswax candles shaped into a hive – with artificial bees fixed in place to complete the look and create a real touch of the country!

SCENTED CANDLES

As well as naturally scented beeswax candles, you can buy candles which have had scented oils added to them, which fill the surrounding atmosphere with their fragrance as they burn. A wide range of scents is available, varying from those with sensuous or romantic aromas to others which create a relaxing atmosphere. You may also find more practical perfumes that can have an invigorating, refreshing or useful effect. For instance, some candles are made specifically to burn in a room where people are smoking cigarettes – they absorb the smoke and leave the air smelling much fresher.

Most scented candles are moulded but you can also buy scented container candles. Although some floral scents can be mixed, before you light a number of scented candles at the same time think carefully about whether the fragrances will go together. There is a danger that if you burn powerfully scented candles, the contrasting fragrances may clash.

GARDEN CANDLES

Using your garden to the full so that it becomes an extension of your din-

Above: *Scented candles.*
Below: *Garden candles.*

ing room or kitchen – eating alfresco or entertaining friends around a barbecue – has become much more fashionable in recent years. Candles are a perfect source of evening or night lighting in the garden, and the range of garden candles on the market is very extensive.

Circumstances dictate that the best garden candles are usually container candles because the flames need to be protected from any draughts and breezes. Terracotta or galvanized metal flowerpots make particularly good containers for candles, especially since they blend so unobtrusively into a garden setting. Container candles can also be hung from the branches of a tree (so long as there is no danger of foliage catching alight). You may be able to find small coloured glass lanterns which can be suspended from above, using wire rather than string which can obviously be a fire hazard. Lanterns are equally effective on an outdoor table because their glass sides also protect the flames.

Many garden candles contain some sort of perfume that will help to keep mosquitoes and midges at bay. Usually this is in the form of an oil that is added to the wax and that the insects find unpleasant.

STAINED-GLASS CANDLES

As the techniques of candle makers have improved, so the decorative surfaces applied to candles have become more adventurous and dramatic. Stained-glass candles are so-called because, as they burn down, the light from the flame glows from the inside out through the wax, in the same way that stained glass is illuminated when rays of sunlight shine through it. These candles, which tend to be spherical, have an almost translucent quality.

Since they are time-consuming to make, with more complicated candle-making methods involved than, for instance, an ordinary dipped candle, stained-glass candles are quite expensive. They are available in many designs and patterns, often to suit a particular season or occasion.

These candles are produced in one of two ways. Either an appliquéd technique is followed during which patterns of solid wax are stuck to the outside of a candle – and this is then dipped to give it a smooth surface. Alternatively, the different coloured waxes which make up the design are inlaid into the wax. One of the most interesting aspects of these candles is the way that some colour schemes and designs can result in the candles looking extremely natural, in some cases even like a smooth lump of stone or a weathered pebble.

SHAPED CANDLES

Candles can be moulded into almost any imaginable shape. Some of the most effective are those that mimic natural forms and are recognizable as objects, but are not necessarily what

you would expect candles to look like. These include cones, chestnuts, hazelnuts, leaves, feathers, twigs and branches that are particularly effective when used in conjunction with a seasonal flower arrangement. Similarly, moulded candles in the shape of small oranges could be displayed alongside a bowl of real citrus fruit. You can even buy novelty-shaped candles, such as a ball of string which is made from interwoven layers of wax – the results are very lifelike! Candles may be created on witty themes, or shaped like children's favourite cartoon or TV characters. These moulded candles are often made in wax with a solid colour but may also have colour painted on to the surface to make the finished result look more detailed and realistic. Perhaps the only drawback with this type of candle is that it is likely to be quite expensive.

CHURCH CANDLES

Church candles have a high proportion of beeswax, so they will burn for a long time. They have been made by the same method for centuries. Originally they were very much a part of

ceremonies in church and the general religious atmosphere, so they bring a little mystery and magical symbolism with them to the home.

Pillared candles come in many sizes and widths, from a standard 15cm (6 in) height up to 90cm (36in). Their classic ivory colouring makes them suit quite heavy black metal candleholders in a Gothic style or those designed to create a medieval feel. Although their beeswax content makes these candles quite expensive, they do burn for longer than ordinary paraffin wax candles.

FLOATING CANDLES

Wax naturally floats in water, so floating candles use this inherent property as a decorative element. Most floating candles are either simple circular shapes or moulded into flowers with broad petals. These look particularly pretty floating on water. You can also buy floating candles with a seaside theme – fish and shells, for instance.

The most effective way to display these candles is to group half a dozen or so together in a bowl, perhaps putting fresh flowers or petals float-

Opposite: *These shaped candles are beautifully crafted and look surprisingly realistic.*
Above: *Church candles come in many different heights and thicknesses.*
Above right: *Themed candles.*
Below: *Floating candles and nightlights.*

ing in among them. Obviously, the water element makes this a safer way to burn candles than some other displays. Also, burning a number of floating candles in this way provides a larger pool of light because the water almost acts like a mirror, and its reflective qualities bounce the flickering light off the surface.

THEMED CANDLES

If you are planning a party of any sort, you can take a theme through to the candles that you use to decorate and light your home. Using colour as a theme is a fairly easy starting point – at Christmas, try using green, red and white or perhaps just sparkling, festive gold. At certain times of the year, you can also buy candles based on an idea or special day like Hallowe'en. A bright orange pumpkin candle or a black candle decorated with a white spider and its web will help to create an effectively spooky, scary atmosphere! Candles moulded in the shape of eggs are ideal for elaborating on the Easter theme.

Just as themed candleholders are often stored out of sight for much of the year, perhaps only putting in an appearance at Christmas or Easter, themed candles should also be enjoyed and burned at the relevant time. Some people just display themed candles without burning them but this defeats the whole purpose of candles. Although they might look pretty when unlit, they only really come to life when their wicks are lit and they flicker and glow.

BASIC
TECHNIQUES

The basic techniques involved in making candles are very simple indeed, and if your first attempts fail, you can put the wax back in the double boiler, melt it and start again. There are several basic techniques, which once mastered, you can use to make candles in any shape or form.

Opposite: *These straight-sided candles show the enormous range of colours in which candles are now available.*

Above: *Dipped candles make good wall decorations even when they are not lit, but make sure that you keep them out of direct sunlight.*

MATERIALS

Obviously the most important material when you are making candles is wax. In the projects the quantity of wax required is not specified because this will vary according to how large a candle you want to make. However, if you are making candles in specific containers the way to work out the quantity you will need is to fill the mould with water and measure it – for every 100ml (3½ floz) of water you will need 90g (3oz) of cold wax. If you melt too much wax this is never a problem because you can simply leave the excess to set and then melt it next time round.

PARAFFIN WAX

This wax is the basic wax used for candle making. It is a colourless, odourless by-product of oil refining. Paraffin wax is generally sold in bead or pellet form and it melts at a temperature between 40–71°C (104–160°F). Often you have to add stearin to wax, but you can buy paraffin wax with stearin already added to it.

BEESWAX

This is a completely natural product which you can buy in its natural shades of brown or in bleached white. It is quite expensive but this is compensated for by its perfume. Generally, it is used in combination with other waxes to increase the burning time of a candle. However, if more than 10 per cent of beeswax is used for a moulded candle you need to apply a releasing agent to the mould first because it has a sticky quality. It is very expensive to make dipped beeswax candles because you need to use a large amount of wax to dip into. If you decide to make dipped beeswax candles, then you do not need to add a releasing agent.

DIP AND CARVE WAX

This type of wax is available in large chunks. It is a blend of waxes which is specially formulated so that it can be carved without it splitting. It has a slightly more malleable quality than ordinary beeswax or paraffin wax. Despite its name, you do not have to use it for dipping candles, although you can if you want.

BEESWAX SHEETS

This is another way to buy beeswax. Beeswax sheets are particularly useful for making rolled candles which are the simplest candles to make because no heat source is required. If you make a tapered candle you will have offcuts. Remember that these can be added to ordinary wax to increase its burning time.

STEARIN

This is used as an additive to paraffin wax to increase its shrinking qualities so that the set wax becomes easier to release when making moulded candles. It also helps to stop candles from dripping. As a guide, you normally need to add about one part stearin for every 10 parts wax. If you add too much stearin, it can affect the appearance of the candle and give it a soap-like finish. If you are making a coloured candle, always add dye to the stearin before you add the wax. When you make a candle, melt the stearin and then add the wax to it.

WICKS

Choosing the right wick for the right candle is essential. If the wick is too small, the flame will be too small. A small wick may also cause the candle to drip, or may be extinguished in a pool of molten wax. The wick itself does not actually burn but it links the vapour from the

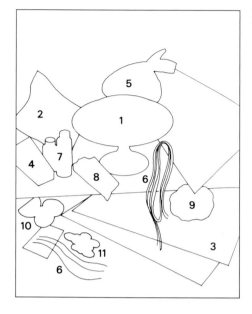

1. Paraffin wax
2. Beeswax
3. Beeswax sheets
4. Dip and carve wax
5. Stearin
6. Primed (right) and unprimed (left) wicks
7. Candle perfume
8. Wax glue
9. Mould seal
10. Wax dye
11. Wick sustainers (wick supports)

molten wax to the flame and it is the vapour that burns!

Wicks should be kept trimmed to 1–2.5cm (½–1in) in length. Usually made from braided cotton, wicks come in many different sizes, ranging from 1–10cm (½–4in) in 1cm (½in) gradations. What size you need depends on the diameter of the candle you are making. You need 2.5cm (1in) wick for a candle 2.5cm (1in) in diameter and so on. You can also buy special wicks for containers, available in small, medium and large sizes for 5–15cm (2–6in). Metal core wicks are specifically designed for longer burning candles and should be used in container candles. Similarly, floating candles require a special floating candle wick.

With the exception of dipped candles, the wick needs to be primed before you make the candle (you can sometimes buy wicks ready primed, but it is easy to do yourself). To prime a wick, melt a little paraffin wax in a double boiler. Leave the wicks to soak in the wax for five minutes – then remove the coated wicks. Straighten them out and leave them to dry on a baking (cookie) sheet lined with greaseproof (wax) paper.

CANDLE PERFUME

Wax perfumes are specifically made to be added to candle wax. You can also use some essential oils but they do not all give off an appealing smell when they are burned. Add a few drops when you have melted the wax, but always be careful not to add too much.

WAX GLUE

This is a soft sticky wax that is available in solid form. To apply the glue, you need to melt only a small amount in the top of a double boiler. You can use it to glue pieces of wax together and also to stick decorations like dried flowers or foil to a candle.

MOULD SEAL

This sticky, putty-like substance is essential for making moulds watertight. It can be re-used many times. Take care to remove any seal from a wick (even a small residue will stop the wick from burning). It is also used to secure the wick in a mould.

WAX DYE

Wax can be dyed to a vast spectrum of colours using wax dyes in disc or powder form. Manufacturers usually give a recommendation as to how much wax an amount of dye will colour, but it really depends on what

shade you want to achieve. If you are overdipping a candle with a coloured wax, the dye needs to be quite strong to be effective.

DYING WAX

Dying wax is very similar to mixing paints. If you are colouring wax by using more than one colour of dye, build the colour up gradually. It is important to note that the colour of molten wax is unlikely to be the colour of wax when set. Some col-

ours are closer to the end result than others. It is a good idea to put a drop of molten wax on to greaseproof (wax) paper while you are melting the wax, so that when it dries you can check on the colour.

WICK SUSTAINERS (WICK SUPPORT)

These are used to anchor the wick in container candles. You push the wick into the sustainer and pinch the metal together so that it will sit flat on the base of the container.

EQUIPMENT

GREASEPROOF (WAX) PAPER

If you have any wax left over when you have finished making your candles, line an old baking pan with greaseproof paper and pour the wax into it. Leave it to set and you can then re-melt it and use it again at a later date.

DOUBLE BOILER

Ideally this should be made of stainless steel or aluminum (it can be enamel coated). You can improvise by placing one saucepan over another, or putting a bowl to rest on a saucepan, but if you do, take special care when measuring the temperature as the wax may melt at an uneven pace.

When using the double boiler, boil water in the bottom of the pan and melt the wax in the top part. Remember to check that the water in the bottom pan does not boil dry, and keep it topped up with more water as necessary. To clean the double boiler, after you have poured out the molten wax, wipe around the inside with a dry kitchen towel.

DIPPING CAN

This tall, cylindrical container is a specialized piece of equipment available from good craft shops and candle-marker's suppliers. It is used to hold the liquid wax and may take more wax than you think it needs. It should be stood in a pan of simmering water, with the level going as high up the sides as possible.

WAX THERMOMETER

When you are making candles the wax must be heated to certain temperatures. You may be able to use a candy or cooking thermometer, so long as its gauge covers the same scale as on a special wax thermometer which is 38–108°C (100–225°F). Never leave wax melting over heat unattended – it can catch alight and is just as volatile as hot cooking oil.

MOULDS

Glass moulds can be used almost indefinitely, so long as you manage not to break them. Plastic and rubber moulds have a more limited life. Plastic moulds tend to be less expensive than glass, and rubber ones more ornate. You can also buy spherical and egg-shaped moulds which come apart in the middle (made out of metal and plastic). Moulds are available in an infinite variety of shapes.

WICKING NEEDLES

These are made of steel and come in various sizes between 10–25cm (4–10 in) long. They can be used for inserting wicks and also for securing a wick at the base of the mould when you wick up before you start melting the wax.

CAKE RING

This is not an essential item in the list of things you need to make candles. However, it is an excellent example of equipment that you may already have in the kitchen which can be adapted to make a mould. For instance, if you fix one side of the ring with mould seal to any sort of base it will be transformed into an instant candle mould.

SPOON OR STIRRER

If you do not have an old spoon, you can substitute it with a wooden stick, but make sure that no splinters can break off and ruin the wax. You do not have to stir wax while it is melting, but you do need to stir when you add dye to it.

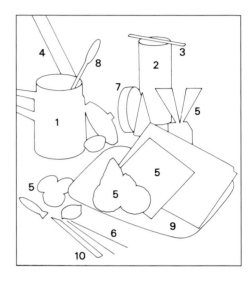

1. *Double boiler*
2. *Dipping can*
3. *Wax thermometer*
4. *Greaseproof (wax) paper*
5. *A selection of rubber and plastic moulds, and small tins which make good moulds too*
6. *Wicking needles*
7. *Cake ring*
8. *Spoon or stirrer*
9. *Baking pan*
10. *Scalpel or craft knife*

OLD BAKING PAN

Apart from using this with greaseproof (wax) paper (see above) when putting leftover wax aside for later use, a baking pan serves as a water bath for cooling small floating candles while they set.

SCALPEL OR CRAFT KNIFE

There are numerous ways in which a craft knife can come in handy when you are making candles. Apart from cutting wicks to length, you can also use it to cut beeswax sheets. When making a template or stencil, you usually get a neater edge if you use a craft knife rather than scissors. Always work with a sharp blade and take care not to cut yourself.

DIPPING CANDLES

Dipped candles are easy to make, with an elegant tapered shape and a unique quality that factory-produced candles cannot match. The candles are made a pair at a time by dipping the wick into a deep can of molten wax. It is extremely satisfying to watch the candles form layer upon layer, gradually building up in thickness with each dip. You can make them in a solid colour or add a coating of coloured wax to white candles by overdipping them. Coated candles have a more intense colour than solid-colour candles and are less likely to fade.

Dipping cans can be bought in various sizes from specialist candlemaking suppliers but an old empty food can (catering size) could be put to good use as an inexpensive makeshift alternative. Dipping cans take a huge amount of wax. The specific amount required will depend on the size of the can but as a guideline a can which is 30cm (12in) high and 13cm (5¼in) wide will need 3kg (6½lb) of cold wax.

HINTS ON DIPPING

For success at dipping candles, using the correct temperature of molten wax is crucial. If it is too hot the previously formed wax layer from the last dip will begin to melt and the smooth finish will be lost. Alternatively, wax that is too cool can result in white marks and lumpy imperfections on the candle's sides. You may need a little practice before becoming totally adept at producing an even dip every time. A final dip in hotter wax at 82°C (180°F) is not essential but gives the candles a lovely smooth finish. Holding the wick so that the pairs of candles are kept apart as they dry can also take a bit of practice as they seem to have an almost magnetic attraction to each other as you lift the tapers out of the wax. Hang pairs held apart over two nails or alternatively over a slat of wood to cool for at least one hour before burning them.

YOU WILL NEED
paraffin wax
metal dipping can
large saucepan
spoon or stick for stirring
wax thermometer
wax dye
lengths of primed wick (see page 72),
    60cm (24in) for each pair of 25cm
    (10in) candles
sharp knife

1 Pour the paraffin wax into the dipping can. Place this in the saucepan and fill the pan with water to reach about halfway up the side of the dipping can. Heat the water to melt the wax, stirring occasionally. Test the temperature of the liquid wax with the thermometer. When it is 71°C (160°F), turn down the heat.

2 To colour the wax, add pieces of solid dye, stirring as you do so to mix the two together well. The dye is usually quite intense, so take care not to add too much. If you want to strengthen the colour after you have made one pair of candles, you can always add more dye to the remaining melted wax, though you will have to reheat.

3 Make sure that the temperature of the wax has not dropped – if it has, bring it back to 71°C (160°F). Hold a length of wick in the middle, and dip the two ends into the wax so that about 5cm (2in) on either side of your fingers remains uncovered. Dip in the wicks in a smooth movement, keeping them in the wax for about three seconds.

4 Leave the dipped wicks to cool for about three minutes. It is a good idea to rig up something that you can hang the wicks over without them touching. Repeat the dipping and drying processes until the candles are the thickness you require – this may take anything from 15 to 30 dips.

5 To give the candles a smooth outer surface, increase the heat of the melted wax to 82°C (180°F). Then dip the candles in the wax for about three seconds, and leave them to cool. When they are cool, trim the bases with a knife so that they are flat. Leave the finished candles to cool for at least one hour before burning.

Right: *Brightly coloured dipped tapers look particularly decorative even when they are not lit. As a dipping can needs a considerable amount of wax to fill it, it is a good idea to make several pairs of candles at a time.*

MOULDING CANDLES

Making moulded candles offers an extraordinary range of possibilities to the candle maker and calls for only the most basic skills to produce professional results. Moulds come in all shapes and sizes, from simple geometric forms such as pyramid, pillar and cube shapes to the more ornate shapes of fruits, vegetables and flowers. They are made of plastic, glass, metal and rubber. On the whole, they are relatively inexpensive to buy and are sturdy enough to be used over and over again. With most rigid moulds (except ones made of rubber), around 10 per cent stearin should be added to the wax to increase the amount of its shrinkage – this will help the candle to slip easily out of the mould. As beeswax is particularly sticky, a release agent should be used on the inside of rigid moulds if more than 10 per cent beeswax is used.

HINTS ON MOULDING

To calculate the amount of wax you will need for a mould, fill the mould with water and measure it – for every 100ml (3½floz) of water you will need 90g (3oz) of cold wax. Most moulded candles start with a primed wick of a grade corresponding to the candle size (see page 72). You will need a length of wick about 5cm (2in) longer than the candle.

Always use plenty of mould seal to make the mould watertight. Some moulds have a base platform or flat end to help stand them upright and steady while others need to be given some support. Rubber and glass moulds with a lipped edge can be suspended through a cardboard collar to hold them vertical.

Where possible use a water bath to help to shorten the cooling time. Candles can be left to cool at room temperature but water cooling improves their appearance. Use a container with a level base and which is roomy enough to fill with water to within 1 cm (½in) of the top of the inverted mould. Always fill the container with water to the correct height before putting the mould in it.

YOU WILL NEED
primed wick (see page 72)
mould
wicking needle
mould seal
stearin (10% of quantity of wax)
double boiler
wax dye
spoon or stick for stirring
praffin wax
wax thermometer
bowl/container as deep as the mould
weight
needle
scissors

1 Thread a primed wick through the hole in the base of sthe mould. Tie the wick around the centre of the wicking needle to hold it firmly at the top of the mould. Then pull the other (burning) end of the wick so that it is taut and press a generous amount of mould seal around it. Check that the mould is completely watertight.

2 Melt the stearin in the double boiler. Then add the dye, breaking the discs into pieces and stirring them in until completely melted.

3 Add the paraffin wax to the double boiler and melt. Test the temperature with a thermometer. When the melted wax is 93°C (199°F), pour it into the *centre* of the mould, taking care not to let the wax splash on to the sides. Leave a gap of about 1cm (½in) at the top of the mould. When the wax has settled for a couple of minutes, tap the side of the mould to get rid of any trapped air bubbles.

4 Fill a container with water, full enough so that when you place the mould in it the water will come to within 1 cm (½in) of the top. Do not let any water splash the wax. Put a weight on top of the mould to prevent it from floating. Leave it to cool for one hour.

5 As the wax dries, a slight dip will form around the wick. Take the mould out of the water bath and prick all over the dipped area. Carefully top up the candle with more wax melted to 93°C (199°F). You need to fill the area around the wick without allowing any wax to spill down the edges of the candle.

6 Let the wax cool in the water bath until completely set and then take it out. When the mould seal is removed, the candle will slide out of the mould. Trim the wick with scissors and then stand the candle in a warm saucepan so that the base of the candle is smooth and level.

Below: *Jewel-coloured star candles and straight-sided pillars are easy to make and look good as a group. The wax has been dyed to give a vibrant range of colours in burnt orange, deep purple and crimson, which look stunning together. Even when candles have a solid steady base, it is best to place them on dishes, plates or tiles while they are burning.*

SCENTED CANDLES

Scented candles fill a room with a delicious fragrance as they burn. A small amount of scented oil or wax perfume added to the molten wax makes all the difference to moulded or dipped candles. You can use the oils produced especially for candle making and available from candle-maker's suppliers or add essential oils, herbs and flowers to give your candles particular qualities, to freshen the air or to create a mood or atmosphere. Aromatherapy oils and plant essences are believed to possess therapeutic powers that can alter mental and emotional states, be soothing, re-energizing and even healing. Choose citrus oils for their uplifting effect, lavender for its calming and antiseptic qualities or sensual ylang-ylang or rose oil to relieve anxiety and tension. Scented candles make extra special gifts as well; you could make fruit-shaped candles as gifts, scenting them with their appropriate fragrance for a novel touch.

USING SCENTED OILS

It is only necessary to add a small amount of scented oil to the molten wax when making perfumed candles; use a dropper to blend nine or ten drops of oil to every kilo (2¼lb) of wax. For moulded candles made with scented wax you will need to use a mould made of rubber or glass, because the oil can damage plastic versions. If you want to perfume a candle made in a plastic mould, you can scent the wick instead of the wax and then make the candle in the usual way. For this method add a few drops of scented oil to the wax when priming the wicks (see page 72). In this project, stearin is not used because it rots rubber moulds.

To calculate the amount of wax you will need for a particular mould, fill the mould with water and measure it – for every 100ml (3½ floz) of water you will require 90g (3oz) of cold wax.

YOU WILL NEED
card (thin posterboard)
bowl
pencil
rubber mould
scissors
primed wick (see page 72)
mould seal
wicking needle
paraffin wax
double boiler
wax dye
spoon or stirrer
wax thermometer
wax perfume or scented oil
needle

2 Thread a primed wick through the mould. Make the end where the wick will burn watertight by blocking it up with a good amount of mould seal. Pull the wick taut and then tie the opposite end of the wick firmly around the middle of a wicking needle.

1 You need a piece of card that is big enough to rest comfortably on top of the bowl which is to be used as a water bath. Draw around the mould on to the card, then cut out the outline. Push the mould into the hole so that the rim at its base is flat against the card.

3 Add the paraffin wax to the top of the double boiler and melt. Add the dye, stirring to mix the two together. Keep testing the temperature of the liquid wax. Heat the wax to 75°C (167°F). When it reaches this temperature, turn off the heat and add a few drops of the perfume or scented oil, stirring it well into the wax.

Above: *This sweetly scented candle is perfumed with rose oil, filling the room with a marvellous fragrance as it burns while also providing a calming effect. The rubber mould used to make it has an ornate Byzantine feel. Rubber moulds are available in more intricate designs than the plastic varieties and include flowers, fruits and vegetables.*

4 Pour the wax into the prepared mould, taking care not to touch the sides. Fill it just as far as the rim of the mould. Now fill the bowl with cold water and leave the candle to cool for one hour. When a dip in the wax forms around the wick, prick the surface with a needle, then add more hot wax to fill the indentation. Leave to cool for another hour.

5 When the wax is completely set and quite cold to the touch, remove the wicking needle and piece of card. Then gently peel back the rubber mould to reveal the candle. Trim the wick at the base and if necessary neaten the bottom of the candle by standing it in a warm saucepan to level off the surface.

CANDY-TWIST CANDLES

Spirals are a classic decorative candle shape and are usually factory-made. However, you can make elegant twisted candles yourself taking hand-dipped tapered candles as your starting point. To twist them, it is simply a matter of flattening each candle with a rolling pin, and then making the turns by hand. They are easy to shape just so long as the candles are kept warm and malleable as you work. These bold spirals bring their own character and rhythm to a mantelpiece or table-setting and only need simple candleholders to show them off. Make short curly candles to add a decorative quality to a severe black metal chandelier, overdipping the tapers in bright vibrantly coloured wax before you twist them.

PRACTICE MAKES PERFECT
You may need to experiment before you can be guaranteed to produce perfect results when twisting candles. Some people find that it is easier to twist a candle if you hold it upside-down, with the wick furthest away from you. As the candles are hand-made, it does not really matter if the twists are unevenly spaced down the candle's length. Even though your first efforts may not be good enough to give away or to display at a grand occasion, the candles will burn perfectly well even if they are not technically perfect. They should not drip – this only happens when the candle is in a draught or if the wax ingredients are wrongly proportioned.

YOU WILL NEED
newly dipped candle (see page 76),
   still malleable
rolling pin

1 Flatten the candle with the rolling pin on a clean, smooth surface until it is about 6 mm (¼in) thick. Try not to flatten the base of the candle (which needs to fit into a candleholder) though, if you do, this can be remedied.

2 Hold the candle near the wick between the thumb and forefinger of one hand and near the base with your other hand. Keeping one hand steady, gently twist the candle with the other. Continue to twist the candle. You need to work quite quickly while the wax is warm enough to respond but do not be too vigorous.

3 When the candle has twists all along its length, check that the base will fit into a candleholder. If necessary, shape it with your fingers so that it is round again. Then leave the candle to cool for at least one hour before burning.

Above: *Tapered candles dipped in yellow ochre, jade green, crimson and ultramarine take on a new twist when shaped into elegant spirals. Hand-twisting them adds a character which sits comfortably in both a classical or contemporary setting.*

ROLLED CANDLES

Rolled candles made from thin sheets of wax are the simplest candles to make. Wax sheets can be bought ready for use and need only to be warm and pliable before you begin. Beeswax has a delicious natural smell and comes in pre-formed honeycomb sheets. It is easy to work with and the attractive embossed surface adds charm to the finished candles. Paraffin wax sheets can be used in the same way but because they tend to be brittle and rather more difficult to work with, they will require extra care to keep them warm and pliable.

To soften the wax sheets and prevent them from cracking, use a hairdryer to warm them slightly. There is no need to prime the wick before you start to make a candle but the burning end of the wick will need to be primed before it is set alight. To do this simply pull a small corner piece of wax from the edge of the sheet and press it around the end of the wick.

YOU WILL NEED
sheet of beeswax
hairdryer
scalpel or craft knife
metal ruler
wick
scissors

Above: *Rolled candles made from white beeswax sheets give a particularly stylish look. Straight-sided candles and spiralling tapers are easy to make but a beehive-shape is slightly more fiddly. First roll a straight pillar around the wick for the centre of the candle, then build up the shape around this, adding bands that gradually decrease in height.*

1 To make a tapered candle, use a rectangular sheet of beeswax and warm it with a hairdryer. The short side of the sheet determines the height of the candle. Cut a narrow triangular segment off the longest side.

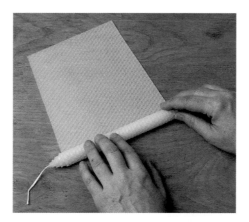

2 Cut a wick which will extend about 2cm (¾in) above the height of the candle. Press the wick gently into the edge of this longer short side. Roll up the wax, checking that the wick is held closely from the first turn.

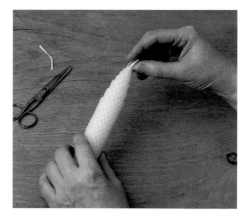

3 When you have finished rolling the wax, press the edge into the candle to give a smooth finish. Trim the wick, then wrap a tiny piece of wax around it so that it is primed and ready for burning.

DECORATIVE CANDLES

Once you have mastered the basic techniques of candle making the possibilities for creating decorative candles are endless. You can either make candles in interesting shapes and colours and patterns, or you can decorate the surface of ready-made candles in any number of ways. Whichever means you choose, you can create some truly stunning candles which will add a sparkle to any occasion.

Opposite: *If you want to give these candles decorated with foils as a gift, follow a treasure chest theme and package them by making a cardboard casket big enough to hold the candles.*

Above: *To paint these uncomplicated designs is within the scope of everyone. A Shaker-style box filled with these stars and stripes candles would make an original gift idea.*

CARVED CANDLES

Carved candles have a wonderful three-dimensional quality and the wax almost looks like carved wood when the candles are lit. Cutting through a deeper dyed outer layer of wax reveals the cream base candle underneath. Although the carving technique is straightforward, requiring only a small amount of practice at making the patterns, the candles do need to be specially prepared to work on. Use ivory church candles or make moulded shaped candles yourself from undyed paraffin wax to form the base. Choose candles with smooth, rounded surfaces to work on and overdip them in deeper country-style colours. Carve through the outer layer of wax using a lino- (linoleum-) or wood-cutting tool to make V-shaped grooves and build up the patterns with designs of feathered lines, stars and flower shapes.

CANDLES TO CARVE

Egg, sphere and pillar candle shapes can be made from undyed paraffin wax in the same way as the moulded candles on page 78. It is a good idea to make a selection of candles at the same time so that you have a few spare to practise on if you are carving for the first time. Once the candles have set and have been removed from their moulds they need to be overdipped to give them a rich outer colour that will provide contrast to the wax underneath.

Melt, dip and carve wax in a dipping can standing in a saucepan of water. The wax will need to fill the can so that it is deeper than the tallest of your candles. Add wax dye to the molten wax until it reaches the required colour intensity. As the colour of molten wax does not accurately show what colour the set wax will

be, it may be helpful to keep a piece of greaseproof (wax) paper close by on which you can put drops of the wax to test how the colour will change as it sets. When the wax is at a dipping temperature of 71°C (160°F), hold the candles by their wicks, and dip them into the wax for about three seconds, allowing them to cool for a minute or two between dips. Dip them two or three times until the outer coating takes on the required intensity, keeping this layer as thin as possible. Set the candles to one side and leave them to cool for at least an hour before you carve them.

YOU WILL NEED

egg-shaped white candle with dipped coloured outer coating
small and large V-shaped lino-cutting tools (linoleum knives)
firm dry paintbrush

1 With the small cutting tool, cut a line from the bottom of the candle to the wick. Begin with a shallow surface line, then deepen it slightly with another cut to reveal the white wax underneath more clearly.

2 Cut small lines branching off the original line at regular intervals to create a feathery effect. Start at the wick and work down towards the base. The best way to ensure that these small lines have a good tip to them is to place the tool the required distance from the long line and work towards it, rather than working from the line outwards.

3 Use a firm dry brush to remove any wax debris as you work. Repeat the feathered line design on the other side of the candle, directly opposite the first one so that the candle's surface is halved.

Above: *Pillared, spiral and egg-shaped candles have been given a deep outer coating in rich country colours especially to embellish with hearts, stars and flower motifs. These simple folk-art designs are ideal patterns to choose for carving. However, particularly when you start carving, remember that straight, tapered lines are much easier to cut than curves.*

4 Cut a star-shaped flower in each of the two halves – the centre of the flower should be midway between the two feathered lines. Cut the shape of the petals lightly at first with the small tool, and leave a circle of wax uncut in the middle of the flower. Then use a larger cutter to define and deepen the petals, and to emphasize their shape.

5 Brush away the wax debris as before. If necessary tidy up the carving using a small cutting tool. The trick with carving these candles is to make the first cut very lightly, and then cut in deeper stages. If the first cut is a deep one, it is likely to chip the outer colour.

STENCILLED CANDLES

Plain candles can be made to look more exciting for a party or in fact any type of celebration with stencils. This is a particularly useful method for producing repeat pattern decorations because, of course, once you have cut the stencil you can embellish several candles in the same way quite quickly. Ivory church candles provide an ideal base to work on but you can stencil on to any candle. Rounded surfaces are, however, very difficult to decorate. It is best to opt for straight-sided pillars or geometric candles. The stencil needs to adhere tightly to the wax surface to give crisp edges around the patterns. Avoid getting paint on the candle wick.

HOW TO STENCIL

You can cut the design out of stencil card (posterboard) or thin plastic sheet, available at craft suppliers, to produce elegant repeat patterns for your candles. Alternatively use bands of lace oddments, or even paper doilies, wrapped around a basic candle to create a delicate filigree design. Metallic spray paints add a glamorous shimmer and can be mixed together in light layers to add texture and interest. Practise spraying the paint first on to waste paper, until you get the hang of it. Always follow the manufacturer's instructions about how to apply the paint and use a light touch – you will be surprised how little you need to give a stunning effect. Spray in short controlled bursts and don't struggle to achieve a perfectly even finish; a slightly uneven texture is almost preferable.

SAFETY WARNING

You should never use spray paints near a naked flame.

YOU WILL NEED
candles
tape measure
stencil card (posterboard)
pencil
ruler
scalpel or craft knife
spray adhesive or masking tape
non-toxic spray paints
lace or paper shelf edging

1 To make a stencil to cover the whole candle, first measure its height and circumference. Then draw your design on a piece of card to fit. Cut out the parts of the design which will form the pattern on the candle.

2 Fix the stencil firmly around the candle. Coat the back of the stencil with a light layer of a spray adhesive that allows for repositioning and stick it to the candle. Alternatively, put a length of masking tape where the two ends meet.

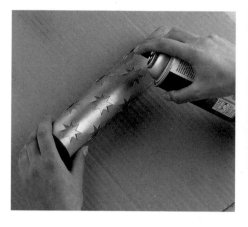

3 Wrap the stencil tightly around the candle and then apply the paint, leave it to dry and remove the stencil.

4 An equally effective method that does not require you to make a stencil is to cut lengths of lace or paper shelf edging to fit around the candle. Fix them in place with masking tape and then spray on the paint. Again, leave the paint to dry before removing the 'stencil'.

Opposite: *Fine layers of gold and silver paint give stencilled candles added shimmer for a special occasion. A harlequin diamond design and simple star and fleur-de-lys motifs will soon transform classically elegant ivory church candles. Here other candles have been decorated with a delicate filigree design stencilled with strips of lace and paper shelf edging.*

SHELL AND SEASIDE CANDLES

Shells can be filled with candle wax to make pretty container candles which have the natural feel of the seaside. They make an unusual memento of beach rambles and an inexpensive, useful present if you are on an economy drive. Oyster shell candles look particularly exquisite when displayed *en masse* among a platter of seaweed or even set among real oysters if you are serving them at an extravagant meal. Always try to use shells with interesting shapes and markings and think about mixing them with fish-shaped candles moulded in tiny baking tins. These candles will float if immersed in water so they offer lots of scope for use as decorations at parties. Display these seaside candles with other bits and pieces that fit the theme such as driftwood, weathered wood and dried seaweed.

PREPARING SHELLS AND MOULDS
If you plan to use shells as containers, or any type of mould, it is essential that they are completely clean and dry before you pour wax into them.

YOU WILL NEED
shells
mould seal
paraffin wax
double boiler
wax thermometer
primed wick (see page 72)
scissors
fish-shaped metal mousse moulds
    and biscuit (cookie) cutters
shallow bowl or plate
stearin (10% of quantity of wax)
wax dye
spoon or stirrer
wicking needle

1 Place the shells on a level surface and use blobs of mould seal to hold them steadily upright. Heat the paraffin wax to 82°C (180°F) in the top of a double boiler and pour the molten wax carefully into the shells, not quite filling them.

2 Leave the wax until it is slightly set – just enough to hold a wick in place. Cut the wick into short lengths with scissors and push a piece into the centre of each wax-filled shell – about 2cm (¾in) of wick should extend above the wax. As the wax shrinks, top up with more molten wax and leave to cool.

3 To make candles in the shape of fish, place the cutters on an old plate or shallow bowl and seal them at the base with mould seal. Arrange the mousse moulds so that they are also level and wedge them firmly in place with more mould seal.

4 Melt the stearin in the top of a double boiler and add the dye, stirring so that it is thoroughly blended. When the dye has dissolved, add the paraffin wax and heat until it reaches 82°C (180°F). Pour the molten wax carefully into the moulds, not quite up to the rims.

5 Leave the wax to set for at least one hour, topping up the wells which form as the wax shrinks. When the wax is completely set, it will come away from the sides of the mould, so the fish can be easily turned out. Pierce the centre of each fish with a wicking needle and push lengths of wick into each hole, ensuring that 2 cm (¾ in) is left sticking out.

Above: *These pretty candles on a seaside theme need only a shallow dish to float in. They will create a relaxing atmosphere whether they are used as a centrepiece on a dining table or anywhere else in the house. If you have space for them in the bathroom, they would also add a romantic, pampering touch while you or your guests enjoy a long, reviving bath in flattering candlelight.*

PAINTED CANDLES

Painted designs worked on to ordinary cream candles can be as simple or extravagant as you like. This is an easy way to make candles look really special and even if you think you have not been blessed with great artistic talent, you can achieve surprisingly stylish results. Keep the pattern simple, and try painting some pillar candles with horizontal bands and others with vertical ones in subtle colours to decorate the table for a dinner party. Or you could combine vertical and horizontal bands to create hand-painted tartan designs. Alternatively go for a bright floral theme and cover candles with blooms and blossoms for summer dining alfresco.

APPLYING THE PAINT

You can paint a candle's surface using water-based paints as well as melted dyed wax and beeswax. Try experimenting to find out which type gives the effects you want and which you like to work with best. The simplest technique is to use water-based gouache or poster paint with a few drops of washing-up (dish-washing) liquid added for a smooth consistency that is simple to mix and apply. The surface of the candle should be clean.

As you work around the candle always take care not to smudge the areas you have already painted. You may find it easier if the candle is standing upright in a candlestick but you should protect this with masking tape or clear film (plastic wrap) to prevent splashing it with paint. When you have completed the decoration, leave the candle until the paint is absolutely dry. If you are making candles to give as presents you can protect the painted design by dipping them in a thin coat of paraffin wax.

YOU WILL NEED
white or cream candle
damp cloth
blue poster paint
fine paintbrush
darning needle (optional)

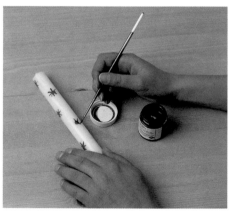

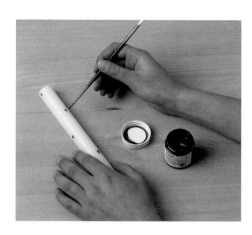

1 Prepare the candle by wiping its surface with a damp cloth and drying it carefully. This will give the paint better adhesion. Mark dots of paint at equal distances over the surface of the candle so that the pattern is regular.

2 Carefully enlarge each dot into a star. It is easier to paint an asterisk and then thicken the lines, rather than try to paint a perfect star freehand. When the paint is dry, if you want to add more texture and dimension, use a darning needle to scratch a spiral in the centre of each star.

Above: *These humble cream candles have been given a touch of country charm by painting them with very simple motifs – bands, dots, and child-like stars.*

DECORATING WITH FOILS

P aper foil used to wrap sweets and candies comes in delicious metallic colours. Rather than throwing them away, you can recycle them along with 'jewels' and beads to add opulent decoration to candles. Look out for candles with metallic finishes in bronze, gold, deep fuchsia pinks and amethyst to provide a colourful starting point.

USING THE FOILS

There are two ways in which you can attach foil to a candle. You can either place foil shapes on to the wax surface and run a teaspoon, which has been heated in steam from a boiling kettle, over the foil. This should be sufficient to melt the wax enough for the foil to adhere. Alternatively, melt a small amount of wax glue and apply it to the back of the foil with a small brush. 'Jewels' can be glued in place in the same way and sequins and beads with holes can be fixed with pins – glass-headed pins add to the jewelled look. Remember to keep this type of candle out of the reach of children's inquisitive hands even when not alight. Also, do not stick foils near the wick because this can interfere with the candle's burning properties and make it difficult to light. As the candle burns down, trim the foil from time to time so that it is level with the top edge.

YOU WILL NEED
scissors
foil wrappers
candle
darning needle
lighted nightlight
teaspoon
wax glue and brush (optional)
sequins
dressmaking pins
gemstones

Above: *Exotic globe and droplet-shaped candles have been embellished with foil bands and shapes, jewels and sequins for an opulent effect.*

1 Cut the foil into strips and shapes ready for use as decoration. Lightly stick the first strip in place by heating the tip of the darning needle in a flame, positioning the foil on the candle and running the needle over it.

2 Alternatively, you can heat the back of a teaspoon in steam from a boiling kettle, or coat the back of the foil with wax glue. Then press the foil firmly in place applying even pressure with the spoon (unheated if you are using glue).

3 Attach sequins to the candle with a dressmaking pin through the centre of each. To fix a gemstone, heat the darning needle in the nightlight flame. Make an indentation in the candle with the hot tip of the needle. Try the gem for size and run the hot needle over the indentation again before pressing the stone in place.

FLOATING CANDLES

All candles float if surrounded by enough water, and small candles made especially to use in this way make use of this naturally inherent property. As well as being an extremely pretty way of displaying the candles there is an added safety bonus, because the water provides some protection when the candles burn down low. A glass bowl can be used for floating a group of candles together, and fresh flowerheads and leaves can be arranged so that they float in between them.

MOULDS FOR FLOATING CANDLES

Metal *petit four* tins make ideal moulds for making floating candles and come in attractive fluted shapes which give the candles a scalloped flowery appearance. Any tin can be used so long as it has a smooth surface and is wider at the top than at the base, so that the candle will slip out easily when it has set. As well as *petit four* moulds look out for other interesting shapes which will produce patterned and embossed details on the candle surface.

YOU WILL NEED

stearin (10% of quantity of wax)
double boiler
wax dye
spoon or stirrer
paraffin wax
wax thermometer
metal *petit four* moulds
old baking pan
weights (optional)
primed wick (see page 72)
scissors

Top: *Tiny shaped candles in vivid colours have the irresistible appeal of a candy store. Group the candles together in a glass bowl or float individual candles in shallow goblets.*

1 Melt the stearin in the top of the double boiler and add the dye, stirring until thoroughly blended, then add the paraffin wax. Heat until the wax has melted and reaches a temperature of 82°C (180°F). Pour it carefully into the moulds and gently tap the sides to release any bubbles.

2 Sit the tins in shallow water in an old baking pan to help them cool, weighting them down if necessary to stop them floating about.

3 When the wax has started to set and a well forms in the centre of each one, re-heat the wax as before and top up each candle.

4 Push a length of wick into the centre of each candle while the wax is still soft but firm enough to hold the wick upright. Leave until completely set, by which time the wax will have shrunk away from the sides of the moulds and the candles can be turned out. Trim the wicks to 1–2cm (½–¾in) and leave the candles for several hours before burning.

SHAKER CANDLES

Candles can be decorated with sponged patterns and motifs cut out of wax for a simple home-spun feel. Biscuit (cookie) cutters come in numerous different shapes, from heart, star and leaf designs to gingerbread figures and farmyard animals, so the choice of motifs is wide ranging.

YOU WILL NEED
sponge about 2 cm (¾in) thick
fibre-tipped pen
scalpel or craft knife
old baking pan
greaseproof (wax) paper
paraffin wax
double boiler
deep red wax dye
spoon or stirrer
heart-shaped biscuit (cookie) cutter
plate
aquamarine water-based paint
washing-up (dish-washing) liquid
candle
wax glue
fine paintbrush

2 Line the baking pan with grease-proof paper. Melt a small quantity of wax in the top of the double boiler and add the dye. Stir until well blended. Pour the molten wax into the lined baking pan. Tip the pan to spread out the wax evenly so that it forms a fine layer. Keep the wax warm so that it remains pliable. While the wax is still soft, use the cutters to stamp out as many hearts as you need.

4 If the wax hearts have hardened, warm them in the oven or on top of a radiator until they are malleable again. Press a heart against the candle so that it becomes curved. Then melt a little wax glue to use as an adhesive. Paint one side of the heart with glue and then press it firmly to the candle. Add more hearts at equal intervals until the decoration is complete.

1 To prepare the sponge for the border design, draw four small squares so that together they make one larger square which looks as though it has been quartered. Cut out half the depth of the sponge on two diagonally opposite squares.

3 Mix the paint with a little washing-up liquid to the consistency of double cream. Dip the sponge into the paint and then press it on to the candle to make a border. When the borders are complete, leave them to dry thoroughly.

Above: *A candle with sponged check borders and a row of appliquéd hearts captures the traditional feel of American country style.*

GOLD LEAF CANDLES

Gold leaf is expensive if you use it in large quantities but it has a special quality all of its own. It can be used to decorate candles to give stunning results. English transfer leaf – the best kind to use for this job – can be bought in books which contain several sheets. If you feel confident, you can draw designs freehand, transferring a pattern directly on to candles. However, although the technique is very easy, mistakes can prove quite costly. If you are trying this for the first time, you are advised to draw your design on paper before you start. The safest method is to trace a pattern on to the gold leaf.

TRANSFERRING DESIGNS

The easiest way to transfer the gold leaf design on to the candle is to trace a pattern on to the gold leaf with a ballpoint pen. To vary the thickness of the gold lines, you could try using a knitting needle or other blunt-ended instrument. Do not use anything with a sharp point that might pierce the paper or gold leaf. Always take care to apply even pressure and press only where you want the pattern to be transferred. The negative pattern left on the used gold leaf transfer sheets need not be wasted and can be re-used to decorate another candle. In this instance, you need to rub directly on the gold leaf (without using tracing paper) so that you can see exactly where the gold remains.

YOU WILL NEED
tracing paper
fibre-tipped pen
sheets of gold leaf
candle
masking tape
scissors
ballpoint pen or blunt-ended
    instrument

1 Draw your design on to tracing paper (the sheets from between the gold leaf transfer are ideal for this purpose because they match the gold leaf exactly in size).

2 Position a sheet of gold leaf transfer, gold side against the candle, and fix it firmly in place with strips of masking tape.

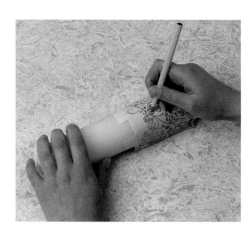

3 Place the tracing paper with your design over the gold leaf. Fix it lightly in place with masking tape so that you can lift it off and reposition it later. Draw over the pattern with a ballpoint pen – there is no harm in embellishing your basic design at this stage if you want to.

4 Peel back the gold leaf transfer, checking that all the pattern has been successfully transferred. If necessary, replace it and trace any parts again.

5 Using fresh sheets of gold leaf, and re-using your tracing paper design, repeat all the above until a gold pattern has been applied all over the candle. As more of the candle becomes decorated try not to stick masking tape on to areas where the pattern has already been applied.

Opposite: *A touch of gold always makes any object seem more lavish – and using gold leaf is a simple way to bring a sparkle to pale cream or white candles. Although the candles here are not coloured, gold can look just as effective against darker colours such as green and crimson.*

MARBLED CANDLES

Wax dyed in rich colours mimics the natural mottling of real marble when kneaded together. Of course, you can just as easily use pale pigment shades for other marble and stone effects in muted yellow and red ochres, blue and cream, or sandy shades with cream for a more neutral look. The wax must be kept warm and pliable and you will need to work quite fast. If the wax begins to harden, place it on a warm oven in a pan to heat it through but do not let it get so hot that it melts.

ROLLING THE WAX

If you want to make a rolled candle with a spiralled top, as this one here, make a paper template in advance. Draw a rectangle on paper 28 × 15cm (11 × 6 in). On one of the two shorter sides, mark two points about 17mm (just under ¾in) in from the corners. Draw a freehand line from these points to the corners at the other end, curving the lines slightly as you do so, then cut along these lines. The size of the template will determine the amount of wax required. For this template, you will need a total of 270g (9½ oz) of wax.

For a candle with straight sides and a flat top and base, trim the edges of the rolled wax into a rectangle before you roll it around the wick.

YOU WILL NEED
dip and carve wax
sharp knife
double boiler
wax dye
spoon or stirrer
2 old baking pans
4 sheets greaseproof (wax) paper,
   larger than pans
rolling pin
paper template (see above)
primed wick (see page 72)

1 Cut half of the wax into chunks and melt it in the top of the boiler. Stir in the dye. Line a baking pan with greaseproof paper so that it overlaps the sides and pour the wax into the pan.

2 Melt the remaining wax and dye it in a contrasting colour. Prepare the second baking pan and pour in the second batch of wax.

3 Leave the wax to set slightly, so that it is no longer runny but is still pliable. Keep it constantly in a warm atmosphere. Roll both lots of wax into sausage shapes between the greaseproof paper, then knead the two contrasting rolls together. The two colours should be mingled but should not be mixed so much that they blend into a single colour.

4 Keeping the wax warm and pliable, put it on a clean sheet of greaseproof paper, on a smooth, flat surface. Cover it with another sheet of paper and then use a rolling pin to roll out and flatten the wax until it is about 5 mm (¼ in) thick.

5 Remove the top piece of greaseproof paper. Place the paper template directly on the wax and quickly cut round the edge with a sharp knife. Discard the leftover pieces or keep them to make into another small candle, depending on how much there is.

6 Press a length of wick along the widest end of the wax so that 2cm (¾in) extends above the top edge.

7 Then roll the wax tightly and carefully around the wick, working away from you.

8 Continue to roll up the wax, keeping it as straight as possible. When you get to the end, press the edge into the candle. Trim the base and the wick. Leave to set for at least one hour before burning.

Right: *If you are a newcomer to making candles, practise mixing small quantities of solidifying coloured wax in a sheet of greaseproof paper before you commit yourself to a whole batch — that way you will avoid wasting wax unnecessarily. As an alternative, you can create a marbled effect by dipping candles into a water-filled dipping can which has coloured wax floating on the surface.*

SAND CANDLES

Nothing can compare with the glowing effect of a sand candle. As the candle burns down the light radiates through the outer layer of sand proving that beautiful candles can be created from the simplest materials. The method is very easy. You use wet sand to make a mould which is filled with molten wax. Different grades of sand provide different textures and colours so it is worth experimenting. You need to keep the amount of water to a minimum so that the sand will stay in shape. Generally 150 ml (¼pt) of water to half a bucket of dry sand is about right. The crusty coating can be shaped and carved with a surface-forming tool or rasp for a more ornate finish.

HEATING THE WAX

The hotter the wax the more it will seep into the sand. Wax heated in the top of a double boiler will not reach a temperature above the boiling point of water (100°C/212°F), so the wax must be melted in an open pan in order to reach the higher temperature needed when making sand candles. Always heat the wax gently and monitor the temperature carefully, so that the wax does not overheat.

SAFETY WARNING

Remember that wax heated to high temperatures can be a fire hazard because it will catch alight if you are not extremely careful. In the event of this happening, treat it in the same way as you would a pan of burning oil: switch off the source of heat immediately and smother the flames with a damp cloth or tightly fitting metal lid. Do not try to extinguish the flames with water.

YOU WILL NEED

damp sand
large mixing bowl
mould such as an ovenproof bowl
primed wick (page 72)
scissors
stearin (10% of quantity of wax)
wax dye
spoon or stirrer
paraffin wax
wax thermometer
metal spoon
wicking needle

1 Pour damp sand into the large bowl so that it is about half full and press it down firmly with your fist.

2 Push the smaller bowl into the sand. Some of the sand will be displaced to rise up the sides. Add more around the edges, pressing firmly.

3 Carefully remove the bowl. Measure the depth of the hole and cut the primed wick to this length adding about 2.5cm (1in).

4 Heat the stearin in the saucepan, add the dye and when it is well mixed, add the paraffin wax. Taking care to watch the wax all the time, heat it to 127°C (261°F) and remove it from the heat.

5 Gently pour a little wax into the centre of the mould, trickling it over the back of a metal spoon so that the sand holds it shape as much as possible. Within five minutes, the wax will seep into the sand, so top up the candle with more wax, again heated to 127°C (261°F). After about two hours, a well will form in the middle of the wax. Top up with more wax.

7 Leave the wax to cool for another three hours, then lift the candle out of the sand. Smooth or shape the candle with a surface-forming tool as desired. Finish by trimming the wick and smoothing the base of the candle in a warm saucepan or with an iron set on medium heat.

Above: *Press a bowl into wet sand to make a mould for sand candles in bold primary colours. If you plan to use them on summer evenings in the garden, or to brighten up a night-time beach party, you could add a few drops of citronella oil to the wax so that the candles become insect repellants as well as sources of light.*

6 Push the wicking needle through the centre of the well and lower the wick into the hole. Wind the top of the wick around the needle and rest the needle across the sand.

101

EMBOSSED CANDLES

Corrugated cardboard can be used to make simple moulds for candle making and gives exceptionally stylish results with a ridged surface to the candles. Spraying the card wet with water or silicone oil spray before you pour in the wax helps to prevent the wax from sticking to the cardboard as it sets. If any card does remain stuck, it is easy to remove. Simply wait until the candle has set and cooled, then hold it under running water and rub away the card with your thumb to leave a textured finish. Try using light and heavy-duty corrugated cardboard to produce a group of candles with different sized ridges, to be displayed together. You could also tie them around the middle with linen tape for an extra decorative flourish still in keeping with the muted style.

MAKESHIFT MOULDS
You could look out for other textured cardboard that would be suitable to make moulds and give an embossed surface to your hand-crafted candles. It is best to use a plastic lid for the base of the mould, and you need plenty of mould seal to make the join watertight where the card meets the plastic. With cardboard moulds the wax should be kept to a cooler temperature than you would normally use when making moulded candles. Generally, if wax is too cool when it is poured, you may end up with an inferior looking candle with white mottling on its surface. With this type of candle these effects are desirable and particularly suit the style.

YOU WILL NEED
clean plastic container lid
bradawl (awl)
corrugated cardboard
scissors
water or silicone oil spray
strong tape
mould seal
primed wick (see page 72)
wicking needle
stearin (10% of quantity of wax)
double boiler
wax dye
spoon or stirrer
paraffin wax
wax thermometer

1 To make the base of the mould, pierce the middle of the plastic lid with the bradawl to make a hole that is big enough to take the wick.

2 Cut a rectangle of corrugated cardboard to the desired size. The width will be the height of the candle and the length will determine the candle's diameter.

3 Spray the card thoroughly with water or silicone oil spray, then roll it into a cylinder and join the sides where they meet with strong tape – something like double-sided tape is ideal for the purpose.

4 To make the mould, place the cardboard roll centrally over the plastic lid. Seal the join with mould seal – the mould needs to be absolutely watertight.

5 Attach one end of a length of wick to the wicking needle, pushing the other end through the hole in the base of the mould. Let the needle rest on the top of the cardboard cylinder. Working from underneath, seal the hole around the wick at the base with mould seal to make it watertight.

6 Melt the stearin in the top of a double boiler and add the dye until it is the right colour, stirring until it is thoroughly blended. Add the paraffin wax to the mixture and heat until it has melted and reached 82°C (180°F). Pour the molten wax into the mould, almost to the rim.

Above: *This type of candle looks particularly good when the wax is dyed a natural honey colour to imitate the colour of corrugated cardboard. The ridged surface of the candle almost makes it appear to be actually made of cardboard. To look its best, the candle needs to be surrounded by natural objects like the pebbles, starfish and cardboard displayed with it here.*

7 Leave the candle to cool. Top up around the wick with more molten wax when a well forms as the wax shrinks. When the candle is completely set, peel off the tape and mould seal so that you can remove the cardboard. Finally, cut off any excess wick.

103

Containers for Candles

TYPES OF HOLDERS

For as long as candles have been used as a source of light, candlesticks and holders have helped to keep them steady and upright. Candleholders and containers play an essential part in the way that candles are used and displayed, serving a practical as well as aesthetic purpose.

It is not necessary to spend a fortune on candle accessories to suit your personal style. It is easy both to adapt existing containers, adding your own personal touch, and to make your own original holders. There is endless scope for ways to enhance the magic of your candle flames to suit any style or theme.

Opposite: *Candleholders range from inexpensive basic designs to those that are much more elaborate and costly.*

Above: *A range of candelabra.*

A Gallery of Candleholders

WOODEN CANDLEHOLDERS

Wooden candlesticks have a sturdy traditional quality which sits comfortably in a rustic setting or a room that is decorated in an ethnic style. Since medieval times, substantial candleholders have been carved out of solid blocks of wood with spikes shaped to hold a thick pillar candle. Some wooden candlesticks, like those made with twisted stems in ebony and mahogany during the seventeenth century, are sought-after collectors' items.

Wood provides an ideal base for further embellishment. A few coats of paint can mimic the passing of time, give a period feel or simply add a splash of colour. Many candlesticks for sale are now imported from Far Eastern countries, where they are produced cheaply. Some of these candlesticks and candleholders incorporate brass ornamentation and rich colour-washed paint effects. The versatility of wood means that it can be turned and carved in the most unusual designs.

CERAMIC CANDLEHOLDERS

Creamware candlesticks have been made by the potteries in England since the eighteenth century. Traditionally the designs include classical pillars as well as more ornate versions which incorporate floral swags and creatures into the pattern. Their tendency to be easily broken means that there are not as many antique ceramic candlesticks as wooden ones.

Today, many contemporary potters and craftspeople are producing unusual, colourful candlesticks decorated with vibrantly painted patterns and glazes. Both commercially produced and individual hand-crafted candlesticks are often made to match tableware, with decorative techniques including sponged designs that suit many interior styles.

GLASS CANDLEHOLDERS

The transparency and sparkle of glass make it a perfect partner for candle-light. Victorian dressing-table sets often included candlesticks in coloured glass and blown glassware has now become highly collectable. These candlesticks often have decorative twists inside the stems, with air bubbles confirming that they have been crafted by hand.

Left: *Wooden candleholders.*
Above: *Ceramic candleholders.*
Opposite above: *Lanterns.*
Opposite below: *Glass candleholders.*

The quality, type and cost of glass candleholders varies dramatically. Sparkling cut glass and lead crystal have wonderful reflective qualities, while coloured glass, like cheap Egyptian glassware in aquamarine, green and amber, has a delicate fragility. Some glass comes in almost naive, irregular shapes. The charm of many of these pieces is that each is different – a one-off.

These days more candlesticks are now being made of recycled glass in either pale green or dyed into vibrant shades. Candle containers in coloured glass come into their own when the candle burns down and the flame glows through the glass.

LANTERNS

Lanterns help to protect candle flames from draughts, making them ideal to hang in the garden – although they can look equally decorative indoors. There is something enjoyable about the ritual of opening and closing the little window on a lantern to replace a candle or to light the wick. Some lanterns have a base that must be unscrewed so that the candle can be inserted from underneath.

The folk art of many countries includes lanterns made in whatever materials are to hand. These lanterns are often crafted out of old tin and other metals, and worked in a naive fashion, incorporating coloured and textured glass as part of the design. Tinware from Mexico, Peru and Morocco often features embossed designs pressed into the metal. Shaker and American country-style lanterns frequently have patterns in punched holes that allow the light from the flame to shine through. Similarly, Oriental iron lanterns with pierced filigree patterns enable light to radiate outwards when the candle is lit.

CANDELABRA

Candles used *en masse* create a dramatic effect as well as giving more illumination. A candelabra always seems to bring more formality to an occasion, more so perhaps it two or more are placed on a dining table. It depends very much on how they are used, though, and they can look just as effective in a less formal setting.

Like all candleholders, candelabra are available in most materials and at prices to suit varying budgets ranging from quality silverware to ethnic wirework and simple metal versions. They are perhaps best placed away from the centre of a room on tables and sideboards so that they do not get in the way. The majority have arms or branches that hold two, three or more candles. Large floor-standing candelbras provide a useful source of lighting on a grander scale – again, they should be positioned so that they cannot be knocked over.

CHANDELIERS

Since chandeliers are suspended from above, they should always have drip trays that will catch melting wax. As an extra precaution, it is best to use them with straight-sided or tapering non-drip candles that have a long burning time.

Chandeliers can be made from almost any material but they are usually metal, wood or crystal. Crystal versions are often expensive but their droplets create a dazzling display when reflecting candlelight. The branches of a chandelier usually swoop or curve slightly down and to the sides, throwing light over a wider area than just a few candles arranged in a small group.

METAL CANDLEHOLDERS

The durability and fire resistant qualities of metal make it an ideal material for candlesticks. It can be turned and twisted, beaten and cast to create splendid hand-crafted shapes. The natural colours of different metals bring their own distinctive qualities to a design, helping to establish a general theme and atmosphere.

For instance, black cast iron has a strength and boldness of line that suits a Gothic decorative style, while pewter and turned brass captures the period feel of Georgian England and a Colonial style. Verdigris copper has a versatility and vibrancy that fits in well with both contemporary and more old-fashioned settings.

SCONCES

These candleholders are fixed to walls, so they are particularly useful if surface space is at a premium. Sconces are most effective in pairs at each end of a mantelpiece, above a bedhead or placed centrally inside alcoves. During the seventeenth century, they were used to line walls and shed light in long dining halls. Many of these sconces had a shiny metal

backplate behind the candle flame which helped to increase the illumination. Later designs often incorporated a mirror in the same way.

Many traditionally styled sconces are still made today in pewter, brass and iron as well as filigree wire designs that will hold coloured glass jars. Although sconces complement a Gothic theme in particular, they may also be used as a light source in a simple everyday environment.

CANDLE SHADES AND ACCESSORIES

Candle shades are primarily used to stop the glare from a candle flame, which makes them very useful at dinner parties – they will allow candles to illuminate the table but not dazzle the guests. Shades have a decorative quality which means that they can easily be used to extend a theme or colour scheme and make the whole table setting look more attractive. They are usually made of metal or card and may incorporate découpage. Many stylish shades are simply and effectively fastened with threaded cord.

Candle shades must always be used in conjunction with shade hol-

Top left: *Chandeliers.*
Top: *Metal candleholders.*
Above: *Wall sconces.*
Opposite above: *Themed candleholders.*
Opposite: *Nightlights.*

ders. These are nearly always made of brass. They hold the shade in place above the flame and are available from interior design and home acces-

110

sory stores. There is a fire risk when any material is close to a candle flame, so always use candle shades with particular care. It is advisable to use straight-sided candles with a high stearin content – they are less likely to soften from the heat of the brass shade holder.

THEMED CANDLEHOLDERS

Lighting candles and using candles in the home is an essential part of many ceremonies and celebrations. Over the years, candleholders have been designed for specific uses and have often developed into decorative objects in themselves. Christmas, in particular, is a time for which candles and candlesticks are designed to fit into a theme. Many sparkling accessories will immediately create a real party and festive atmosphere.

Christmas tree candleholders hold small straight-sided candles. Some simply clip on to the branches while others hang from them. The stems of the hanging type are weighted so that the candles will stay upright. It is possible to obtain these in Shaker style, made of tin, with cut-out heart shapes which add an extra decorative element to the tree.

SNUFFERS AND ACCESSORIES

Snuffers and snuffing scissors are an integral part of the tradition of using candles. Snuffers serve a practical purpose and all designs are variations on the traditional cone shape. When a snuffer is held over a lighted candle it stops oxygen feeding the flame which is quickly extinguished. Snuffers are available in many different styles and shapes – but they should be made of metal so that there is no danger of them catching alight. After use, you can leave out more decorative snuffers on display.

Snuffing scissors have a particular period feel to them and antique versions have now become collectable

items. They should be used by applying the small flat metal 'blades' in a scissor action on to the part of the wick that is alight so that it is squashed. This puts out the flame.

Other useful candle accessories include a box to store supplies of candles. Many are available including versions in black punched metal in American folk art style. Glass nuggets or marbles are a useful decorative addition to water containers that

you might float candles in. Candle sharpeners are made to fit straight-sided candles. If a standard candle is too big for a candleholder, you can use a sharpener to shave thin strips of wax off the base.

Candle fix, supplied in small tins or as flat beads in packets, is a soft, sticky wax which is applied to the bottom of a candle. It prevents candles from wobbling around in a dangerous fashion because it holds them firmly upright.

NIGHTLIGHTS

Nightlights burn for a long time and are reasonably safe compared to other candles. Putting them in small glass cups and containers protects the flame – those in coloured glass will also throw colourful light on to a scene. If you want to hang nightlights, perhaps from a tree in the garden, use wire rather than string which might catch alight.

Nightlight containers are often made in weathered steel or brass with small patterned holes punched into the sides to let light through. Most nightlights are circular but it is possible to buy them in flower and star shapes.

ADAPTING CONTAINERS

Nothing is more satisfying than transforming a container that was about to be thrown away into a decorative object for your home. It is often not until you put your mind to how to adapt everyday household items, such as jars, bottles, tins and glasses, that you realize their potential. With one coat of paint they can be given a second lease of life and turned into unique and colourful candleholders.

Opposite: *As the candles burn down, the metal surface of these containers will give an extra glow and make the perfect accompaniment for dining out of doors on summer evenings.*

Above: *New wooden candlesticks can be painted to give the impression that you have had them for years.*

MEDITERRANEAN CANDLE CANS

I t is really simple to transform old cans into excellent containers for candles. Numerous suppliers in Mediterranean countries package different foodstuffs in richly decorated and lavishly patterned cans, which can be put to good use after their contents have been consumed.

MAKING CONTAINER CANDLES

For this type of candle it is important to use special container wick (stiff wicking) which will stay alight as the wax melts. Choose the wick size to correspond to the diameter of your container (see page 72). If you add beeswax to the paraffin wax, the burning time will be lengthened. A few drops of citronella oil added to the melted wax will act as an insect repellant, helping to ward off unwelcome mosquitoes and midges.

SAFETY WARNING

The wax will liquefy as the candles burn, making the containers very hot, so always take care to place metal container candles on steady surfaces and out of children's reach.

Check that the cans are watertight and fill any holes with a blob of mould seal. Make sure that the cans are clean and dry and that the lids have been removed neatly to leave a smooth edge. To calculate the amount of wax required, fill the mould with water and measure it − for every 100ml (3½floz) of water you will need 90g (3oz) of cold wax.

YOU WILL NEED

container wick (stiff wicking)
clean can for container
wick sustainer (wick support)
pencil or wicking needle
paraffin wax
double boiler
wax thermometer

1 Using a length of container wick several inches longer than the container, push one end through a wick sustainer, pressing the metal together around the wick to secure it. Tie the other end around a pencil so that the sustainer rests on the bottom of the can and the pencil rests on the rim.

2 Melt the paraffin wax in the top of a double boiler. Test the temperature of the liquid wax with the thermometer. When it reaches 82°C (180°F) remove it from the heat.

3 Pour a small amount of wax into the can and hold the pencil and wick in place until the end of the sustainer is fixed in position by set wax. Pour in more wax, a layer at a time, so that the wax around the sustainer remains set and the wick stays in position.

4 Pour in more melted wax to within 1cm (½in) of the rim of the tin and leave the wax to set. A well will form around the wick as the wax sets and shrinks. Reheat the wax and top up the container with more melted wax as necessary. Unravel the wick from the pencil and cut it down to size.

Above: *Capturing the essence of hot, balmy holiday evenings, brightly decorated cans make splendid container candles. As the candles burn down, the metal surface of the containers will give an extra glow. You can refill the cans with new wax again and again.*

MAKING USE OF BOTTLES

A candle pushed into an empty wine bottle has become something of a cliché on tables in restaurants, bistros and wine bars, but the practice can be adapted and used to stunning effect to make stylish displays in your home. A solitary old wine bottle is best left for the café table but, for a more dramatic effect, groups of bottles in varying heights and shapes, and with different sized necks to hold thick or thin candles, can be arranged together to illuminate windowsills and alcoves. This is an excellent way to recycle bottles, giving them a second lease of life. Any wear and tear on old bottles often adds character and interest to the glass, frosting the surface in a desirable way.

Alternatively, you can buy new bottles made from recycled glass of greenish tones, mixing squat chunky shapes with taller elegant ones. With a vast selection of recycled bottles now available, you should not be restricted for choice. You may be able to find bottles with embossed designs of grapes, flowers, swirls and facets, adding decorative detail to your display.

A deliberately simple treatment such as a row of clear bottles filled with cream candles can give a look of utilitarian chic while plainer bottles might benefit if a little extra interest is added. The bottle necks can be wrapped with gold cord finished off with tassels, or tied with bows of colourful ribbon or simple linen braid. You might also be inspired to fill bottles with small shells or tiny glass nuggets. Or tor a special occasion, you could fill bottles with water coloured with food dye. You can achieve a back-to-nature effect by twining fresh foliage and flowers around and among the bottles. You can even create a bottle display in miniature by using old perfume bottles with small Christmas tree candles pushed into their necks. The list of possibilities is endless.

Below: *A collection of old bottles makes a splendid arrangement on a windowsill when used to make impromptu candlesticks. The candles are not identical but come from within a limited colour spectrum to give a unified look.*

BYZANTINE JAM JARS

It is particularly pleasing when you are able to adapt very simple materials into a stunning display. Even ordinary jam jars can be decorated with stained-glass paints to make a dazzling range of candleholders with a Byzantine feel. Stained-glass paints are available in a rich transparent colour range that look good used together, especially when shimmering in candlelight. You can adapt the jars to make hanging lights by winding gold cord and tassels around the rims. It is possible to burn any candles inside jam jars but nightlights are the safest alternative.

PAINTING THE JARS

Wash old jars in warm soapy water to remove any grease and residue from the labels. Use lighter fluid or a similar solvent to remove particularly obstinate blobs of adhesive. Make sure that the jars are completely dry before you begin. Stained-glass paints are easy to work with. They have a viscous texture which will run slowly down the surface of a jar to cover it evenly. However, take care

not to let heavy drips build up because the paint dries quickly – most of the brushmarks will vanish as the paint dries. Make sure that the transparent colour is completely dry before applying the decoration. If you are going to apply an embossed outline, it is worth practising in advance – the technique is like icing a cake and the paint can run out of the nozzle quite quickly when you first begin. Experiment with swirling and zigzag patterns, highlighting the edges of the panels, as well as single dots.

Below: *Large jar candle lights are a simple way to bring light into the garden on summer evenings. To protect the candle flames from draughts, partly fill the jars with sand. Then push candles down into the sand so that they are standing upright and firmly in place.*

YOU WILL NEED
glass jam jars
stained-glass paints
flat bristle paintbrush, about 1cm
　(½in) wide
outline paint

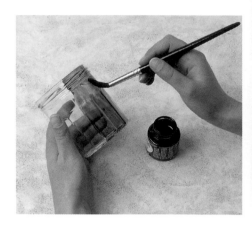

1 Paint the outside of a clean jam jar with undiluted stained-glass paint. Be quite generous with the amount you apply but take care not to let drips form. Leave the jar to dry completely, which should take about 24 hours.

2 Work out your design for the decorative pattern, then gently squeeze the outline paint directly from the tube nozzle on to the painted surface of the jar. Try letting the paint flow evenly. When you have finished, leave the jar to dry. It should be touch-dry in about 24 hours but needs to be left for another 48 hours or so until it has set hard.

Opposite: *Look out for jars in varying shapes and sizes with flat faceted sides or other features which you can highlight.*

PAINTED CANDLESTICKS

New wooden candlesticks can be aged and mellowed using simple paint techniques which instantly give a patina of age. One way to create a simple antique finish is to pick out the grooves in a candlestick with roughly painted contrasting bands of colour worked in two close shades to accentuate the curves in the shape. Look out for candlesticks with grooves and twists which will benefit from this kind of treatment. By applying an antiquing patina to the fresh painted surface, you can age the candlestick with just a few brushstrokes. The effect is intensified if the surface is rubbed back to the wood in places, with any extra knocks and chips further enhancing the distressed look. A craquelure (crackle) finish (available from specialist shops) makes a fine network of tiny cracks all over the surface, again creating a desirable aged effect. With this finish, refer to the manufacturer's instructions on how to achieve large or fine cracks.

PAINTING CANDLESTICKS

Natural wood or previously painted candlesticks are perfect to work with. There is no need to remove the old paint completely, just make sure that the surface is clean, dry and oil-free before you start. Sand the surface lightly with fine sandpaper to remove any old varnish and make the surface smooth. Wipe away any dust that results.

Opposite: *A craquelure finish and simple antiquing paint techniques can be used to make new candlesticks look antique, if not hundreds of years old. The effects of ageing are easy to mimic – with patience, paint and varnish you can create the dirt and grime, knocks and scuffs that normally take years to accumulate and which look so appealing.*

FOR ANTIQUE-FINISH CANDLESTICK

YOU WILL NEED
wooden candlestick
wax candle
off-white emulsion (latex) paint
small, flat and fine paintbrushes
fine sandpaper or steel wool
antiquing patina
rag
acrylic paints (smoke blue and jade green)
matt (flat) varnish
varnishing brush

1 Rub the candlestick with the candle, applying a light coating of wax to any pointed edges and areas which would be most likely to be damaged through wear and tear.

2 Paint the candlestick with off-white emulsion and leave to dry. If the wood shows through the paint, apply a second coat and leave to dry thoroughly.

3 Lightly rub over the painted candlestick, using fine sandpaper or wire wool, to give a scuffed surface. Take the paint right back to the original wood in a few places.

4 Apply a coat of antiquing patina with a brush. Lift off some of the patina with a rag to mellow the painted surface and add texture.

5 Using a fine paintbrush, roughly paint bands of smoke blue around the top and bottom of the candlestick as well as inside any grooves. Don't worry about being too careful and precise – uneven edges on the bands give the best effect. Leave the painted candlestick to dry.

6 Roughly paint thin lines of jade green within the smoke blue bands. Leave to dry thoroughly then brush on a coat of matt varnish to finish.

118

FOR GOLD CANDLESTICK

YOU WILL NEED

candlestick
gold paint
paintbrushes
craquelure (crackle) base varnish
craquelure (crackle) varnish
antiquing wax or raw umber oil
    pigment
soft cotton cloth
matt (flat) varnish
varnishing brush

1 Paint the candlestick gold, taking care not to let the paint build up in any grooves. Spread the paint with even, regular brushstrokes. It is better to apply two thin coats if necessary rather than put on a thick initial layer of paint. Leave the paint to dry thoroughly.

2 Brush on an even coat of craquelure base varnish. Brush it out smoothly so that no drips form.

3 Let the varnish dry naturally – this should take about 15–20 minutes. For a fine cracks effect, you may need to apply a second coat. Leave it to dry completely. Next, use a clean, dry brush to apply an even coat of crackle varnish to the entire surface, making sure that the base coat of varnish is thoroughly covered.

4 Smooth out the varnish and put the candlestick aside to dry naturally (this will take about 15–20 minutes). Colourless cracks will form over the surface. Take a cotton rag and rub a little antiquing wax or oil pigment into the cracks. Wipe away any excess wax or pigment and then seal the surface with a coat of varnish.

FOIL LEAF CHANDELIER

To add a decorative flourish to plain candlesticks, candelabra and chandeliers, thread metal foil leaves on to soft wire so that they reflect an extra glimmer in the candlelight. You can make the lengths of the leaves as long or as short as you like. Either wrap the leaves around the candlestick or – for a more ambitious design – all along the arms of a chandelier. You can also add a finishing touch to the chandelier by bunching leaves to make a tassel at the base. Different coloured metals can be used together, alternating the colours, or you can opt for a single colour with wire to match the leaves. You need a dressmaker's tracing wheel to make leaf vein patterns on the soft foil surfaces of the leaves.

USING METAL FOIL

Metal foil is available from some specialist craft suppliers in small sheets or you may be able to buy it from metal merchants. The metal needs to be thin enough to take a pattern when applied with a dry ballpoint pen and to be cut easily with scissors. Small embroidery scissors are a worthwhile investment if you plan to make several foil items.

YOU WILL NEED

pencil and paper for template
thin card (posterboard)
scissors
foil – aluminium, copper and bronze,
   .003in thick/40 gauge
chinagraph pencil (china marker)
small pointed scissors
protective gloves (optional)
dressmaker's tracing wheel
bradawl (awl)
soft copper wire, 1mm (1⁄16in)
   diameter
chandelier

1 Size up the template of the oak leaf on page 156 and transfer it on to thin card. Cut this out and place it on a piece of metal foil. Draw around the template with a chinagraph pencil.

2 Remove the template and cut the leaf shape out of the foil with small scissors. Take care not to cut yourself on the sharp edges of the foil. Take your time over this step and trim away any rough edges as necessary.

3 Produce the pinprick lines to create veins on the foil leaf, using a dressmaker's tracing wheel. You will have to press quite hard to make the impressions in the foil. You may find that it helps if you work on a slightly yielding surface, such as a magazine.

4 Make more leaves out of the different foils in the same way. Then punch a hole with the bradawl in the stalk end of each leaf. Don't make the hole too big – just large enough to thread the leaf on to the wire.

5 Cut a length of wire long enough to wind around one of the arms of the chandelier. Thread the leaves on to the wire, alternating the metals.

6 Twist the wire around one arm of the chandelier so that you have a secure starting point. Then wind the wire around the chandelier, releasing a leaf every 8–10cm (3–4in). Make sure that the end of the wire is tightly secured before starting with another length of wire. Wind around more lengths of wire with leaves until it is completely decorated. Hang three or four leaves under the centre of the chandelier as a finishing touch.

Right: *An oak leaf chandelier makes a focal point for any living room and would look splendid hung above a dining table. The shiny foil leaves are easy to bend and arrange – giving a feel of spontaneity and opulence to the simple lines of the original plain black chandelier.*

121

TASSELLED CHANDELIER

A cheap metal chandelier has been given a new lease of life by binding it with twine and embellishing it with tassels and beads. String and paper cord are everyday materials which can be used to produce exceptionally stylish results, with the natural colours and textures becoming an important part of the overall design. You could decorate other styles of chandelier in the same way. Choose chandeliers with a simple structure to begin with and then let inspiration take over!

DECORATING A CHANDELIER

Try a combination of coloured string and paper cord with richly coloured beads for an alternative look. Or experiment with a horticultural theme. For instance, you could hang miniature watering cans from each arm with green garden twine. Glass fruit Christmas tree decorations look stunning used to decorate a chandelier, especially if you are fortunate enough to find antique ones. Another variation is to bind a spray-painted metal chandelier loosely with upholstery cord so that the metal shows through. Then hang fancy ready-made tassels in complementing colours underneath the candleholders.

YOU WILL NEED
corrugated cardboard
scissors
paper cord
string or twine
scalpel or craft knife
gold thread
beads
PVA (white) glue
simple metal chandelier
spray paint (optional)

1 To make each tassel, cut two similar rectangles of cardboard – the length of the card should be the length you want the tassels to be. Put the two pieces of card together and wind paper cord around them. The more cord you use the thicker the tassels will be. Thread a piece of paper cord, twine or string between the rectangles, pull up and tie tightly at one end to make the top of the tassel. Cut through the cord at the other end with a craft knife.

2 Remove the pieces of cardboard and bind the tassel with gold thread 3cm (1¼in) down from its top, tying the ends tightly. Slip another length of gold thread through the top of the tassel, thread a bead on to it and tie a knot to hold it in place.

3 Make matching tassels for each candleholder on the chandelier and a slightly larger one with a bigger bead to hang centrally from the bottom.

4 Starting from the central core of the chandelier, glue the end of the string to one of the arms. Wind the string around the arm, gradually working towards the holder and completely covering the metal. When you reach the holder, cut the string and glue the end in place, holding it firmly until it has stuck.

5 Cut a small strip of cardboard to fit around each candleholder. Glue the cardboard in place, then wind string around from the bottom to the top of the cardboard until it is completely covered. Cut the string and glue the end at the top.

6 Cover all the arms and candleholders with string in the same way, followed by the central core. If the chandelier has push-in candleholders, give them a coat of spray paint and glue them in position when dry.

7 Some chandeliers have a weighted ball underneath to keep them steady. If you are decorating one of this type, you need to cover the ball with string. First, glue the gold thread holding the bead at the top of the large tassel around the weighted ball. Beginning from the bead, spiral and glue string around the ball until it is completely covered.

8 Hang the chandelier in place then tie or glue a tassel beneath each candleholder.

Right: *A simple wire chandelier takes on a completely different style when decorated with everyday materials, tassels and beads. The natural shades of paper cord and twine have been used to turn it into something extraordinary, even though the materials used to decorate it are quite mundane.*

DECORATIVE HOLDERS

Candleholders can be made using
a wide range of craft techniques
and materials, and each project in this
chapter utilizes a different method to
create a unique candleholder which can
be used as a basis to make further
more elaborate variations. In all cases,
it is essential that the candle is carefully secured in the holder before it is
lit. Candle stickers, which are purpose-
made discs of wax, will hold the candle
firmly in place.

Opposite: *These unique papier-mâché leaf*
candleholders are cheap and easy to make.
Once you have mastered the technique,
you can vary the shapes or decoration.

Above: *Pieces of driftwood can be made*
into a simple tripod stand to hold a candle.
Lashed with twine to hold them together,
worn hollowed-out shells are the only
embellishment required.

MOSAIC CANDLESTICK

Mirrored mosaic is a perfect accompaniment for candlelight. The faceted surfaces will catch the glow of a flame and send out reflections in all directions. Mosaic patterns can be made from all types of waste materials and are an excellent way of recycling broken bits and pieces. Although the ingredients you need are humdrum, the resulting effect is remarkably stylish. Mirrored mosaic wall tiles consist of numerous rectangular mirror pieces, attached to a mesh backing. The backing helps to hold the pieces in place when you need to break them into irregular shapes. You should also be able to find small circular mirror pieces (which look good when incorporated into a mosaic) in ethnic shops.

As well as using pieces of mirror to cover candlesticks and candleholders, you can make other matching accessories to use alongside them. The more items decorated with mosaic that you display together, the more dramatic the overall effect will be when the candles are lit.

SAFETY WARNING
Do remember to take care when handling broken glass shards, and wear protective gloves if you can work effectively with them on.

YOU WILL NEED
scalpel or craft knife
mosaic mirror tiles
dish towel or similar old cloth
hammer
protective gloves (optional)
powdered tile adhesive
table knife
candlestick
small round mirror pieces
gold acrylic paint
medium and fine paintbrushes

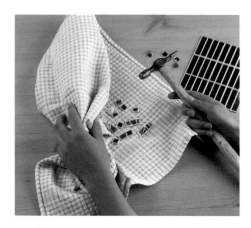

1 Use the craft knife to cut through the backing of a mirror tile, and wrap a segment in the cloth. Break up the mirror into smaller pieces with the hammer. Take care not to cut yourself on any sharp edges – it is advisable to wear protective gloves.

2 Following the manufacturer's instructions, mix up the tile adhesive with water to form a fairly thick paste. Apply the adhesive to the candlestick with a table knife, working on small areas at a time. While the paste is still wet, stick on fragments of mirror and the small round pieces of mirror. Continue until the whole candlestick is covered.

3 When the adhesive is completely dry, use the medium paintbrush to paint the larger areas of white with gold, taking care not to cover the pieces of mirror. Load just the tip of the brush with paint and try to keep your hand as steady as possible.

4 Use a much finer paintbrush to fill in any gaps around the edges of the pieces of mirror. Leave the candlestick to dry and if necessary apply further coats of paint.

Opposite: *Broken mirror pieces transform a basic candlestick into a glittering object of beauty. Here, a bracket wall shelf has been given the same treatment with mosaic edging and gold paint. Arranging mirrored mosaic accessories around a candlestick adds to its impact in the glimmering candlelight.*

RUSTIC CANDLE POT

Dried flowers and grasses make a luscious collar in muted shades around the base of a church candle with an old terracotta plant pot providing a steady pedestal base. This particular design includes bunches of aromatic dried lavender and bay leaves as well as bundles of twigs and grass stems, but there is no limit to the combinations of dried materials you can use.

SAFETY WARNING

Flowers and foliage with wispy and wayward inclinations are best avoided as this type of material in combination with candle flames could be a potential fire hazard. It is safer to use a candle with a high beeswax content which will be long lasting and slow burning. Always keep an eye on the candle while it is alight, and make sure that the flame is extinguished before it reaches the level of the dried plant materials.

YOU WILL NEED

dried flowers, including foliage and
    grasses (6–8 varieties)
flower cutters or secateurs
stub (floral) wires
sharp knife
oasis (dry foam)
flowerpot
hay or straw
florist's tape
candle
mossing pins (optional)
moss

1 First wire the flowers and foliage into small bunches, with four to six stems in each bunch. Cut the stems to about 12.5–15cm (5–6in) and hold the flowers firmly in one hand. Pass a stub wire behind the stems so that the wire and stems are at right angles to each other. Wrap about 4cm (1½in) of one end of the wire around the stems once.

2 Turn down the end of wire that you have wrapped around the stems so that it is pointing towards the base of the stems. Now wrap the rest of the wire three or four times firmly around the stems to hold them together, covering the other end of the wire as you go, and taking care not to apply so much pressure that they break. You will need six to eight bunches of each variety.

3 Trim the foam to fit inside the flowerpot. Place it in the pot so that about 7.5cm (3in) of the foam stands proud above the rim. Pack hay or straw around the foam to provide a solid base for the candle.

4 Stick a piece of florist's tape all around the base of the candle. Then hold three mossing pins or bent stub wires against the tape and tape over them to hold them in position. Stick the candle into the foam and trim the foam, rounding off the corners.

5 Add the wired bunches, sticking the stub wires into the foam at an angle. Work with one variety at a time and place the bunches all round the candle to get an even balance of materials. If necessary, wire up a few more small bunches to fill any gaps.

6 Finally, fix moss around the base of the candle with bent stub wires or mossing pins, making sure that it is pinned down well.

Above: *Candle pots can also be made using nuts, fir cones and moss for decoration. For best results with these types of pots choose a candle that is in proportion to the pot and hold it well in place with plenty of damp moss pushed all around it.*

Right: *An old weathered terracotta flowerpot provides the base for a lush arrangement with rustic appeal. The cream church candle provides dramatic contrast with the selection of surrounding dried flowers and foliage. Under no circumstances should this arrangement be left unattended when burning.*

129

SEASHORE CANDELABRA

Some of the best materials for making candleholders are completely free. When walking along a beach, keep your eyes open for weathered driftwood, colourful pebbles, pretty shells and smoothed nuggets of glass to take home. These beachcombing finds can be made into stunning candleholders which capture the essence of happy days by the sea. In this yacht candelabra, frosted glass fragments worn away by sand and sea have been strung on to wire to make the 'sails'. A beached starfish is easily made into a candleholder by hollowing out a hole at the centre large enough to fit the candle, the star shape making a good firm base. Alternatively, you could make a jam jar lantern. Wrap wire around the top of a jar and form a handle, threading it through pebbles to decorate the rim.

YOU WILL NEED
driftwood
drill
5 pole supports
small screws
screwdriver
handsaw
glue gun
fragments of glass and pottery
  smoothed by sea
thick and fine copper wire
pliers
3 small hooks
seashells
candle stickers (optional)

Opposite: *A candelabra made from flotsam and jetsam captures the fun of beach walks. This yacht made from driftwood and china and glass fragments holds two candles which when lit make the glass sparkle. A candleholder made from a beached starfish adds to the seaside feel, holding a single candle steady.*

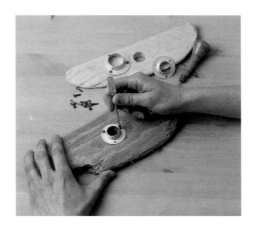

1 Select two flat pieces of wood – one for the base and the other for the candle support. You also need a fairly sturdy stick or pole for the mast. Drill holes the same diameter as the mast through both flat pieces of wood. Screw one pole support over each hole.

2 Take the flat piece of wood which is to be the base and attach the bottom of the mast to the pole support. Fix it firmly with a small screw and glue if necessary. Cut the wood for the mast to the length you require, and push it through the hole in the candle support. Fix it firmly as before. Screw the three other pole supports on to the candle support.

3 To make the 'sails', twist the glass and pottery fragments between two lengths of thick wire, and bind them in place with thin wire. You need two 'sails', long enough to hang between the top of the mast and the ends of the candle support.

4 Finish off the 'sails' with wire loops. Screw one hook into the top of the mast and another at each end of the support. Slip a loop from each 'sail' over the hook at the top of the mast and then over the hooks at either end of the support.

5 To complete this unusual candlestick, decorate the wooden support by gluing on shells. Then put the candles in the pole supports – use candle stickers to hold them firmly if they are not a perfect fit.

COPPER SCONCES

The materials used to make these ingenious flower wall sconces are an unconventional collection of everyday items found in kitchen accessory shops, hardware stores and craft outlets, but the results are far from makeshift. Each sconce is made from a copper mousse mould, metal foil and copper pipe, with a mirrored centre providing additional reflected illumination from the lighted candle. As an extra feature, you can lightly burnish the foil petal edges by holding the metal flower with tongs over a flame. When you are considering what would make suitable copper moulds, try to find shapes that candles will fit into snugly and use candle fix to keep candles firmly and safely in place.

YOU WILL NEED
terracotta-coloured and standard
    epoxy putty
small copper mousse mould
copper reducer to fit pipes 16mm to
    10mm (⅝in to ⅜in) (available
    from plumber's merchants)
pencil and paper for template
thin card (posterboard)
copper foil – .005 in thick/36 gauge
copper-coloured indelible marker
scissors or tin snips
protective gloves (optional)
craft knife
pliers
self-adhesive backed round
    mirror (available from car
    accessory shops)
thin copper pipe, 8mm (⅜in)
    diameter and 30 cm (12in) long
bending spring to fit copper pipe
rolling pin
drill or bradawl (awl)
used matchstick
epoxy adhesive
heavy duty double-sided sticky pads
copper foil adhesive tape (optional)

1 Mix equal parts of the epoxy putty and knead together until it is well blended and copper coloured. Place a good-sized blob of putty on the base of the copper mould and push the reducer into the putty to join them. Leave to dry.

2 Size up the template on page 156 and transfer it on to thin card. Mark the area of copper to be used then draw around the template on to the copper foil, using an indelible marker. Cut out the flower shape with scissors or tin snips and remove the centre circle carefully with a craft knife, keeping it for later use. Take care not to cut yourself on the sharp foil edges.

3 Score lines down the centre of each petal and crease the metal lightly along these lines. Gather and pleat the foil loosely around the central circle, using pliers where necessary, until the flower is three-dimensional and the petals are cupped. Colour the edge of the mirror with indelible pen so it matches the copper.

4 Place the copper circle behind the flower centre. Peel the covering off the back of the adhesive pad on the mirror and fix the mirror to the copper circle so that the flower is sandwiched between them.

Right: *The warm tones of the metal and the reflective qualities of the mirrored flower centres give these sconces a feeling of great charm. To make a larger sconce simply scale up all the materials. To match these holders, you can use small brioche pans to hold single candles. Put them by each place at the dinner table.*

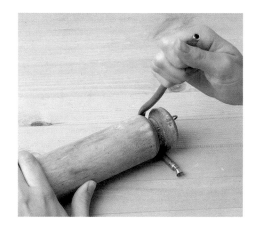

5 Insert the bending spring inside the copper pipe. Hold the rolling pin steady with one hand and bend the pipe about a quarter of the way along its length. Bend the pipe until it forms a curved hook, then remove the spring.

6 Flatten the end of the longer part of the pipe with pliers to form a flat surface on which you will be able to stick the flower. Use a drill or brad-awl to make a hole 1 cm (½in) from the end of the flattened part.

7 With a used matchstick, apply epoxy adhesive to the reducer and stick it to the round end of the length of copper pipe. Leave until it has completely set.

8 Stick the copper flower to the flattened part of the pipe, leaving the hole free for hanging, and using heavy duty double-sided sticky pads (the sort that you might use to fix a mirror to a wall). Cover the joins with strips of copper foil adhesive tape if you want to neaten the back.

BYZANTINE CANDLESTICK

Polymer clay is a versatile material which is available in a multitude of colours. After the clay has been moulded it can be baked in a domestic oven to form a resilient material. This hand-modelled candlestick has been decorated with many segments of multi-coloured spirals and rolls, which embellish the candlestick in a convincing mosaic effect.

WORKING WITH POLYMER CLAY

Before you start to roll the clay, knead and warm it with your hands so that it is easier to work. You are aiming to build up one central cane from several different colours of clay. You can reduce this cane down in size by rolling it, and slicing off segments at different stages. These slices can then be pressed on to the candlestick to create an intricate pattern. Try to apply even pressure as you roll the clay and be confident with your movements. If a log of clay becomes too thin, you can always roll it up, knead it a little more and start again.

SAFETY WARNING

Do not heat the clay above 120°C/250°F/Gas ½ because it releases toxic fumes at a higher temperture.

YOU WILL NEED

rolling pin
polymer clay (purple, yellow, turquoise, white and black)
blade
wooden base which will withstand low heat (120°C/250°F/Gas ½), such as salt shaker
sandpaper

Opposite: Mosaic slices made from rolls of different colours of polymer clay decorate the candlestick to give a jewelled effect with a charming delicacy.

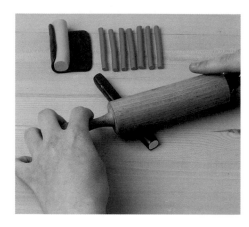

1 Roll out a rectangle of purple clay and use it to cover a log of yellow clay. Also, roll out six thin turquoise logs.

Next cover a white log with a sheet of black clay and then square it off by gently rolling it on four sides. Cut this log in half lengthwise on the diagonal to make two triangular logs, then cut the two halves in half again. You need six black-and-white logs so repeat this process.

2 Place the black-and-white logs and the turquoise logs around the purple log. Wrap this in a sheet of black clay to create a composite cane.

3 Using the blade, slice this cane in half. Set one half aside, then carefully roll the other half between the palms of your hands and a smooth table surface to reduce the diameter.

4 Keep reducing the cane, slicing it in half, then reducing it again until you have several canes of different diameters. If you create really tiny canes, you can join them together. Slice the canes into sections approximately 2.5mm (⅛in) thick.

5 Lightly sand the base – the surface needs to be rough. Mould some black clay into a cup shape at the top of the base to form the actual candleholder. Cover the middle section with a sheet of black clay. Then apply a layer of the slices of clay, working from the bottom up and pressing them on firmly and smoothly.

6 Bake for 30–45 minutes at 120°C/250°F/Gas ½. Leave to cool and then complete the decoration forming a raised pattern. Bake as before.

COPPER CANDELABRA

Plumber's suppliers sell pipe and joints which can be linked together to make a splendid candelabra. This unusual three-candle candelabra is made from copper plumbing parts and decorated with glass marbles. The joints and elbow connectors which are glued to form the shape are all bought separately. For safety reasons, it is obviously important that the candelabra has a good firm base; filling the base with sand helps to make it more stable. Left to weather naturally, the copper will mellow to an attractive finish. But if you like the gleam of shining copper, polish the candelabra regularly to retain its shining appearance.

PLUMBER'S MATERIALS
Plumber's pipes and fittings come in many different gauges, but the basic connectors available are similar. This means that by following the instructions for this candelabra you can make larger candlesticks, going up to floor-standing sizes if you like, simply by using bigger gauge pipe and connectors. Plumber's suppliers also sell pipe in other metal finishes, so it is worth having a look to see what options are available.

YOU WILL NEED
ruler or tape measure
pipe cutter
copper pipe
5 copper reducers to fit pipes 19mm to 16 mm (¾in to ⅝in)
6 T-connectors
6 elbow connectors
3 straight couplings
rapid drying epoxy adhesive
used matchstick
cross connector
funnel
sand
marbles

1 Using the pipe cutter, cut the copper pipe into sections as follows: 1 × 10cm (4in); 1 × 9cm (3½in); 3 × 6.5cm (2½in); 1 × 5cm (2in); 13 × 4 cm (1½in); 2 × 3cm (1¼in).

2 To make the two outer candleholders, arrange the bits you need in this order, using 4cm (1½in) lengths of pipe: reducer, pipe, T-connector, pipe, elbow connector, pipe. For the central candleholder use a reducer, pipe, T-connector, pipe, straight coupling and pipe.

3 When you have got the bits in the correct sequence, glue them in place, using a matchstick to apply the glue and arranging the T-connectors so that the holes are facing forwards (this will be the front of the candlestick).

4 To make the base, glue a T-connector, with the hole facing upwards, to a 6.5cm (2½in) pipe, then add an elbow connector, a 4cm (1½in) pipe, an elbow connector and another 4cm (1½in) pipe. Repeat on the other side of the T-connector. Now glue a 5cm (2in) pipe between the last two T-connectors. Add a 3cm (1¼in) pipe and a reducer to the hole in each of these T-connectors which are pointing upwards. Then glue this section into the front of the base.

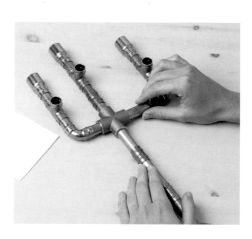

5 To make the central stand of the candelabra, glue the pipe and bits as follows: 10cm (4in) pipe, straight coupling, 9cm (3½in) pipe, straight coupling, 6.5cm (2½in) pipe. Then glue the end of the last short length of pipe and the three candleholders into the cross connector.

6 Use a funnel to pour sand through the hole in one of the T-connectors at the base. Shake the base from time to time to distribute the sand evenly.

7 Glue the top and bottom sections of the candelabra together, providing support at the back and front to ensure that it dries in an upright position, with the T-connectors at the front parallel with the candle stand and candleholders. Glue marbles on to the visible T-connector holes as the final decorative touch.

Right: *The burnished tones of copper pipe and coloured glass marbles reflect the flickering glow from the candles in this stunning three-candle candelabra. Although you need patience to make this creation, it is extremely satisfying to produce such an elegant result out of simple utilitarian materials.*

GARDEN CANDLEHOLDERS

Plant an instant border of dazzling flower candleholders in bright metallic colours for summer garden parties and alfresco dining. The materials are cheap and easy to find – metal foil pie dishes are transformed into shimmering flower heads, with green garden stakes making the flower stems. The flower petals will provide just enough protection for nightlights so that the flames will not be blown out in a summer breeze. You can push the flowers into the earth in a herbaceous border, or use them to light a path or walkway. Alternatively, large flowerpots filled with earth or sand are useful containers for them on a paved patio area or they can be arranged in bunches around a patio table. Foil bowls on small plates and saucers can be further decorated with circles of fresh summer flowers arranged around them. A bouquet of flower candleholders would make a welcome, if unconventional, gift.

YOU WILL NEED
indelible markers
deep-sided foil pie dishes (pans)
scissors
stained-glass paints
paintbrush
small foil pie dishes (pans)
brightly coloured foil sweet (candy)
   wrappers (optional)
epoxy adhesive
nightlights
large flat-headed 2.5cm (1in) nails
medium green garden canes (stakes)
foil flan dish (large pie pan) (optional)
foil strips (optional)
heavy duty double-sided tape
   (optional)

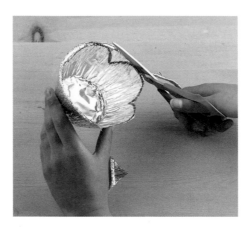

1 Draw the outline of rounded petals on the inside of a foil pie dish with an indelible marker. Cut along the line with scissors so you are left with a flower shape.

2 Paint the flower, inside and out, with stained-glass paint in a bright, vibrant colour. Leave it to dry thoroughly. Repeat all the above to make more candleholders, painting them in single contrasting colours.

3 Cover a small pie dish with bright foil if available, smoothing out the foil and wrapping it over the rim to hold it secure. Alternatively, paint the container with stained-glass paint in a colour that will stand out against the petals already painted.

4 Glue the metal surround from a nightlight into the pie dish. Then stick the pie dish inside the flower and push a nail through the centre point of all three layers to hold them together.

5 Push the nail point into the pithy hollow at one end of a garden cane to fix the assembled flower to it. Add a blob of glue to the joint to hold it all firmly together. When the glue is dry, put the candle into the centre of the flower.

6 If you want to make leaves, mark a flan dish into eight segments with a green indelible marker. Draw two curves between the lines along the rim to make heart shapes. Cut out the segments – each will become an individual leaf.

7 Attach a thin folded strip of foil to the underside of each leaf with heavy-duty double-sided tape. Paint the leaves on both sides with stained-glass paint. Stick the leaves to the cane flower stems with another piece of double-sided tape.

Right: *A garden path lined with bright candle flowers will add a decorative touch to a summer garden party as well as illuminating the walkways as dusk arrives. Alternatively, you could use individual flower heads to decorate place settings at the table.*

WIRE CRAFT CANDLEHOLDERS

Baskets and decorative accessories made from wire mesh have a fabulously elegant feel to them but can be quite expensive to buy. Chicken wire is available from most hardware shops and, despite its robust quality, is surprisingly easy to work, offering plenty of scope for experimentation. You will need to practise for a while to become adept at manipulating the mesh, but once you've mastered the basic technique you will be able to make all types of weird and wonderful candleholders.

WORKING WITH CHICKEN WIRE
Chicken wire comes in many different gauges – try to find a fine mesh that can be easily moulded and bent. A pair of round-nosed pliers is an essential tool – you can obtain these from jewellery maker's suppliers and hardware shops. Protect your hands with gloves if necessary.

YOU WILL NEED
chicken wire
ruler or tape measure
wire cutters
protective gloves (optional)
round-nosed pliers
pliers
flat-headed pins (from jewellery
  maker's suppliers)
droplet beads
large metal bead
epoxy adhesive
wire mesh spoons (1 large, 1 small –
  from oriental shops)

Opposite: *Once you have mastered the simple technique you can form chicken wire into elegant candleholders, candlesticks and shimmering beaded domes.*

1 Cut a piece of chicken wire 30cm (12in) long by 38cm (15¼in) wide and curve it round to form a cylinder. Join the sides by twisting the wire ends together and pushing the sharp points inside the cylinder, using round-nosed pliers.

2 Working around the cylinder, remould each honeycomb shape in the mesh into a heart, using round-nosed pliers. To do this, put the ends of the pliers into each honeycomb and open them so that they push the mesh sides slightly apart. Then tweak the top side of the shape into a 'V'. To do this, position the pliers on the right side of the top horizontal wire of a shape and turn your hand in towards the centre, twisting the pliers around the wire. Reverse for the other side and this will create a heart shape.

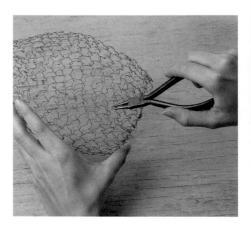

3 To mould the domed shape, working around the cylinder draw the mesh together by degrees towards the bottom and top. The heart shapes will become long and thin where the mesh is pulled in and short and wide around the middle. Continue to refine the shape until the top is tightly drawn together and the base pulled in but still open enough to sit firmly and contain a candle.

4 Pull the top tightly together by applying pressure with the pliers. Squeeze the wire, turning the dome as you go, so that the squashed wire is more rounded than flat.

140

5 Push flat-headed jewellery pins through beads and cut off any excess, leaving just enough wire to twist round into a fixing loop.

6 The beads should hang from the 'V' in the top of the heart shapes. Finish off the top with a metal bead with a large hole. Push the bead over the mesh and apply a blob of adhesive to secure.

7 To make the stand, remove the handles from the wire mesh spoons. The dome will sit on the large wire spoon and the smaller one is for the base of the pedestal.

8 Now cut a piece of chicken wire 13cm (5in) wide by 6.5cm (2½in) deep. Form into a cylinder in the same way as before, then mould the cylinder by pulling the mesh together in the middle to draw it in. Open the mesh at both ends so that it splays out. Join the mesh to the rounded side of the larger metal spoon by twisting the wire ends around the mesh at the centre. Join the other end of the chicken wire stand to the underside of the small spoon in the same way.

PAPIER-MACHE LEAF CANDLEHOLDERS

Brightly painted leaf candleholders are a pleasure to make with papier-mâché pulp which dries to a durable finish. The leaves are painted freehand in a spontaneous style and then distressed slightly to give a mellow worn look. Following the same technique you could vary the shapes to make suns and stars with ridged rays. Several coats of gesso, applied before the painting is done, make a smooth porous surface to take the paint.

SAFETY WARNING
Use wax candle stickers to fix the candles firmly in place if they are not a perfect fit and always extinguish the flames before they reach the level of the holder.

MAKING PAPIER MACHE
You can make paper pulp by boiling torn up newspaper in water until the paper disintegrates. Then you need to squeeze out the excess water, and pulp the paper in an old blender. Add equal parts of fine sawdust, PVA (white) glue, and powdered interior filler, along with a smaller amount of wallpaper paste (without fungicide). Knead the pulp to a working consistency, adding more water if it is too dry or a little interior filler if the mixture is too wet. Store the pulp in clear film (plastic wrap) until you need it. Proprietary papier mâché pulp is available ready to mix with water. To use the pulp simply follow the manufacturer's instructions.

Several coats of gesso applied to the papier mâché before painting gives the surface a firm, smooth finish. Acrylic gesso, which is available ready to use from specialist artist's suppliers, gives good results.

YOU WILL NEED
paper and pencil for template
corrugated cardboard
scalpel or craft knife
metal bottle cap
PVA (white) glue
kitchen knife
papier-mâché pulp
wallpaper paste (without fungicide)
newspaper
gesso
paintbrushes
acrylic paints
fine sandpaper or steel wool
wax polish
rag for polishing wax

1 Size up the leaf template on page 156 and draw around it on to corrugated cardboard. Cut out the shape using a scalpel or craft knife. Place the bottle cap in the centre of the leaf and draw around it. Cut out the circle without cutting completely through, and remove the top layers of cardboard.

2 Check that there are no pieces of card or plastic inside the bottle cap and that it is clean. Then glue it securely into the hole with PVA glue.

3 Using a kitchen knife, build up the pulp on the cardboard leaf so that it is level with the bottle cap at the centre and slopes down to the edges, making a ridge along the middle of each lobe down to the tip of the leaf. Leave the pulp to dry.

4 Paste a layer of newspaper torn into small pieces (lightly smeared on both sides with wallpaper paste) over the leaf's surface and down over the edges and underneath so that it is covered on all sides. Leave the leaf to dry completely.

5 Apply 3 or 4 coats of the gesso with a paintbrush, covering the whole surface of the leaf. Allow the gesso to dry thoroughly between coats.

6 Paint the leaf with acrylics and leave to dry. Emphasize the ridges on the leaf by alternating dark and light colours.

7 Distress the paint finish by rubbing the leaf with very fine sandpaper or steel wool to take small areas back to the gesso. Wipe away any dust.

8 Polish the leaf with furniture wax, leave to harden for a while, then buff it to a satin finish with a soft cloth.

Right: *Brightly painted leaf candleholders with all the charm of folk art, make a stunning table centrepiece, especially when mixed with real leaves. The shape of the leaves can be varied but should be kept simple. Arranging rounded oak leaves alongside pointed leaf shapes makes an effective contrast. Take great care not to let the candles burn so low that they become a fire hazard. Extinguish the flames before they reach the holder.*

FILIGREE CANDLE CROWNS

Metallic candle crowns surround and protect the flames and make pinprick patterns of light through punched holes as the candles burn down inside them. You could place a group of them on a circular tray or platter, or sit single pieces on individual brass dishes or saucers, surrounding candlesticks or holders. Try experimenting with different patterns of pierced holes in straight lines and curly swirls. For further embellishment, glass nuggets and beads set into the metal take on a jewel-like quality with candlelight behind them. To fix them in place, cut holes slightly smaller than the nuggets; spread glue around the holes and press on the glass or beads.

YOU WILL NEED
copper foil, .005in thick/36 gauge
pencil
ruler
protective gloves (optional)
round lid or coin for template
bradawl (awl)
magazine or pile of newspaper
small pointed scissors
brass paper fasteners (paper clips)

Opposite: *Make your candle crowns in different sizes and metals if you plan to arrange them in a group. Coloured glass nuggets glued in place over small holes cut or punched into the foil can be used as additional decorations – they will shimmer prettily when the candlelight glows through them.*

1 Cut a rectangle of foil 28 × 16cm (11 × 6½in). Use a sharp pencil and ruler to draw a line across the length of the foil, dividing it in half. Then draw parallel diagonal lines across the width of the foil, to make a lattice design. Using a round lid or a coin as a template, draw circles between the parallel lines along the top and the bottom edges.

2 Begin to punch holes, regularly spaced, along the pencilled lines, using a bradawl. Punch a single hole in the centre of each circle and triangle. If you like, place a magazine, or something similar, which will 'give' slightly and protect your work surface, underneath the foil.

3 Cut along the top edge with scissors to leave a small border around the punched holes and make a scalloped rim.

4 Gently bend the foil round so that the ends overlap slightly, to form a cylindrical candle crown. Make three corresponding marks on both pieces of foil where they meet and punch holes through these. Push a paper fastener through each set of holes to hold the foil in place, opening out the ends of the fastener on the inside of the crown.

NIGHTLIGHT CHANDELIER

Nightlight candles burn for hours and, as they are enclosed in a metal casing, there is no danger of wax dripping. Also, as they are relatively inexpensive, they are ideal to use in a chandelier – hung over a table the candles will provide a flattering light throughout a long supper party. To make a more ornate chandelier for a special occasion, you could twine ivy around the metal rings and chains, or perhaps hang cords and tassels underneath the chandelier for a more opulent look.

GLASSES AS CONTAINERS

Small drinking glasses, just the right size to take nightlights, are easy to find in clear, coloured or frosted glass. You need nine glasses to attach around this double-tiered candelabra, and four or five more if you want to make a really grand three-tiered version. To save expense, you could recycle small glass food jars. Paint them with stained-glass paints if you want to add some colour.

YOU WILL NEED
2 cake rings, 25cm (10in) and 18cm
  (7in) diameter
tape measure
pencil
bradawl (awl) or drill
green water-based paint
paintbrush
9 glasses to hold nightlights
thin card (posterboard)
scissors
old tin, preferably rusty
tin snips
protective gloves (optional)
18 paper fasteners (paper clips)
epoxy adhesive
metal chain, preferably brass
wire cutters
10 'S' links
round-nosed pliers

1 Measure the circumference of the large cake ring and divide this into six equal sections, marking each sixth with a line. Using the bradawl make two holes in the centre of the ring, 1.5cm (⅝in) either side of each line. You will have 12 holes – these are for the nightlight holders. Repeat this for the small ring but you only need three pairs of holes.

2 Next make holes to hang the chains on. On the large ring, punch three equidistant holes close to the top edge of the ring. On the small ring, punch three holes close to the top edge, and three more directly below these but close to the bottom edge.

3 Paint both rings, inside and out. Leave the paint to dry thoroughly.

4 To make the holders for the glasses in which the nightlights will sit, make a template from thin card for the tin bands. For a glass with a 18cm (7in) circumference the bands need to be about 20 cm (8in) long and 2cm (¾in) deep. Adjust the size to fit the glasses you have. Draw the template with gentle curved sides and rounded corners. Cut nine bands out of tin using tin snips. It is advisable to wear protective gloves.

5 Make a hole with a bradawl at both ends of each band – they should be centred and 6mm (¼in) in from the ends. Bend each band just over 1cm (½in) from its ends and curve the central part around a glass to shape it.

6 Take one band and place it over a pair of holes on the large ring. Push a paper fastener through each hole. Apply epoxy adhesive to the underside of the band. Flatten the paper fasteners on the inside of the ring.

7 Fix the other eight holders to the rings in the same way. As you work, check that the glasses will fit into the holders and do not fall through.

8 Cut three equal lengths of chain with wire cutters and attach an 'S' link to each end. Open up the link with a pair of round-nosed pliers so that you can attach the chains to the three holes along the top rim of the large ring. Attach the other ends of the chains to the holes along the lower edge of the smaller ring.

9 Cut three more equal lengths of chain and attach them to the top edge of the small ring using 'S' links in the same way.

10 Join together the three chains at the top edge of the small ring by threading them through an 'S' link. Attach a length of chain at this point for hanging as required. Paint over the fasteners and touch up any scratches in the paint. Then position the glasses in their holders and add the nightlights.

Below: *A two-tiered chandelier makes a dramatic focal point over a table with amber, blue–green and mulberry coloured glasses holding nightlights. The shade of green paint on the rings gives the chandelier a patina of age, while the rusty holders complete the look. You could always paint the tin in a terracotta or rust colour if you can only find new metal.*

BRAIDED CANDLEHOLDER

Salt dough is a cheap and versatile medium made from ingredients that you will find in your kitchen cupboard. Flour, salt and water mixed into a malleable dough can be shaped, baked and painted to last almost indefinitely. This candleholder has a charming rustic feel and is made with interwoven braids of dough forming a circular base. If you like the natural colour, you can simply finish it off with a few coats of varnish, but you could just as well paint the baked piece.

WORKING WITH SALT DOUGH
When baking salt dough, you need to allow about one hour for every 6mm (¼in) thickness of dough, so drying out usually takes several hours. Once baked, the dough should be golden brown and lift easily from the tray. Press the underside at the thickest part to make sure that it has hardened. If the dough is not dry all the way through, it will continue to dry after varnishing and the candleholder will shrink and crack. You should also leave baked dough until it is cold before you start to paint.

YOU WILL NEED
2 cups plain (all-purpose) flour
1 cup salt
water
clear film (plastic wrap)
shallow round 15cm (6in) ovenproof
    dish with wide rim
baking parchment
cooking oil
rolling pin
6cm (2½in) round pastry cutter
modelling tools
matt (flat) varnish
varnishing brush

Opposite: *A salt dough candleholder.*

1 To make the dough, stir the flour and salt together with sufficient water to make a firm but pliable mixture. Knead by hand for 10 minutes. Cover with clear film and chill in the fridge for one hour.

2 Line the dish with baking parchment and coat with a thin layer of oil. Roll out the dough to about 5mm (¼in) thick, and cut a circle for the foundation of the candlestick.

3 Roll the remaining dough into 'sausages' about 7.5mm (⅓in) thick and cut into lengths of about 15cm (6in). Arrange 16 around the centre circle of dough at regular intervals, leaving sufficient space for a candle in the middle. Press the dough gently in place. Then add another 16 lengths between those in the first layer.

4 To make the base of the candlestick, weave the lengths of dough. Working in pairs, place each alternate roll over the one next to it.

5 Continue to interlace the rolls, placing every other one over the adjacent roll. Work all round the dish and repeat twice.

6 Using a modelling tool, trim the end of each roll and tuck under to form a neat rim. Make the candleholder from two short rolls of dough formed into rings and placed centrally, one on top of the other.

7 Bake the candlestick in the oven at the lowest setting for at least six hours or until it has dried out. Finish off with two coats of varnish – include the base as well.

PAINTED FLOWERPOTS

Terracotta flowerpots have a chunky, robust quality which makes them ideal for holding candles. Use them in their natural state to make impromptu container candles for alfresco evenings, entertaining family and friends in the garden. If you are going to use them indoors, a quick lick of paint will transform pots into dazzling decorations for a table or mantelpiece. Pots can be painted very simply with bands of geometric patterns which are not difficult to achieve. A coating of gold paint inside the pots is what really makes them come alive in the candlelight, giving a shimmering amber glow as the candles burn down. Give old pots a good clean before you paint them, and always check they are dry before you start. When you have applied one layer of paint, leave the pot to dry thoroughly before adding the next coat.

YOU WILL NEED
flowerpots
acrylic paints (yellow, gold and blue)
flat and fine paintbrushes

Right: *Flowerpots painted gold on the inside shimmer in the candlelight.*

1 Using a broad flat brush, paint the pot yellow inside and outside.

2 Paint the inside of the pot gold – one coat should be sufficient.

3 Using a very fine brush, decorate the outside of the pot with blue paint.

FANCY CANDLE COLLARS

Candle collars can be used to add decoration to a candlestick as well as serving a useful purpose, to catch any drips of wax that might run down the candle. For these candle collars, metal foil, cut into flower shapes, is punched, pleated and embossed to make pretty relief designs with beaded droplets added to give a touch of elegance. To catch the drips, the collars should curve up slightly towards the candle and sit snugly on top of the candlestick.

YOU WILL NEED
paper and pencil for template
aluminium foil, .005in thick/
   36 gauge
protective gloves (optional)
chinagraph pencil (china marker)
small pointed scissors
cloth or magazine
dry ballpoint pen
a selection of beads
silver flat-headed pins (from
   jewellery suppliers)
wire cutters
small round-nosed pliers

Above: *All of these collars are worked on the same basic shape. The brass collars with lines of punched holes radiating from the centre are pleated gently all the way round. Alternatively, use beads to make a decorative circlet around the centre of a copper flower, held in place by fine wires threaded through them to the underside.*

1 Size up the template on page 156. Place the template on to a piece of foil and draw around it in chinagraph pencil. Cut out the flower and remove the central circle. Take care not to cut yourself on the sharp foil edges.

2 Lay the flower right side down on a slightly soft surface, such as a folded cloth or magazine. Draw a circle at the base of the petals and veins on the petals themselves with a dry ballpoint pen, pressing hard to make a good impression.

3 With the pen make evenly-spaced dots to fill the centre of the flower. Remove the soft surface, then make a small hole at the end of each petal with the tip of a scissor blade.

4 Thread beads on to silver flat-headed pins and trim the wire, leaving enough to fix to the flower. Thread each wire through the tip of the petals and bend over to secure.

151

STORAGE BOXES

If you light your home with candles all year round it is useful to keep a supply of replacements, especially when a candle chandelier or candelabra is used regularly. Storage boxes are a practical way to keep your candles and the other candle accessories you may need, and they can be displayed as decorative items in themselves.

A brightly lined card and fabric box with a hinged lid can be made to hold a dozen or more candles. Finished off with a taffeta ribbon tie and a tassel, the box could be filled with brilliantly coloured candles to make a stylish and useful gift which looks equally at home on a mantelpiece, shelf or side table. If you adapted this fabric-covered box, you could easily make it without a lid so that you can keep the candles on show all the time. Then you could put it on display, hanging it on a wall with a cord or lavish picture bow looped over a hook.

TINS AND BOXES

A metal box is simple to customize with different shaped compartments to fit candles, tapers, matches and nightlights. If you want to give the box as a present, gather together all the candle accessories you plan to include before you begin and choose your container to fit them. As well as different types and sizes of candles, you might like to add a decorative candle snuffer or a pair of snuffing scissors. A stock of nightlights is always useful, especially coloured or scented ones, as well as candle fix, a candle sharpener and matches.

If you prefer, you could opt for a natural look by making a box from corrugated card, decorating it with cream twine and filling it with beeswax candles.

YOU WILL NEED
paper and pencil for template
card (cardboard)
ruler
scissors
craft knife
fabric to line the box
PVA (white) glue
coloured paper
felt for the base
ribbon
tassel

1 Enlarge the template on page 157 and trace it on to card. Go over the traced lines of the pattern with a pencil and ruler so that the box outline is quite clear.

2 Cut out the box with scissors, then score along the remaining lines as necessary.

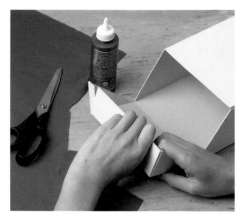

3 Again using the template, cut out the fabric, adding an extra 2cm (¾in) along the edges of the box and lid. Fold up the sides of the card and glue all the flaps to form the box and lid. Hold firmly until it is well stuck.

4 Position the box on the wrong side of the fabric, carefully lining up all the edges. Then glue the fabric to the box, folding and sticking the extra fabric on to the inside.

5 Cut out four pieces of card with which to line the box. The card for the front panel should be 5mm (¼in) higher than the box at the front, as should the side panels – they should graduate down to the same size as the box at the back. Cover all the pieces with coloured paper.

6 Again using the template, cut out a lining for the lid from coloured paper, adding an extra 2cm (¾in) along the edges and fold neatly. Glue all the panels inside the box and the paper inside the lid.

7 To complete the box, cut a rectangle of felt to fit the base of the box and glue to the outside. While this is drying, cut two lengths of ribbon long enough to tie into a bow when the box is shut. Glue the ribbons to the front of the lid and the box. Finally, thread a tassel on to the lower ribbon.

Above: *A lidded box, covered with fabric and lined with contrasting paper, makes an attractive storage box for candles as well as other things. A ribbon tie and a tassel provide extra decoration. In this case, bright candles have been chosen to complement the colours and complete the look.*

Beside it, the sturdy metal box, with corrugated cardboard partitions, is another excellent container for holding accessories and candles, which ideally should be stored flat.

CANDLE SHADES

Candle shades are a delightful way to enhance the light from candle flames and eliminate any unwanted glare, particularly at a dinner table. Pairs of candlesticks with matching shades can add a tasteful symmetry to a mantelpiece or console table. You can leave your shades plain or add decoration to suit any style, binding eyelets along the rim with twine or ribbon, adding patterns with paint and découpage, or embellishing with ornate touches using tassels and rosettes.

SAFETY WARNING

It is absolutely essential that you think about safety when you are using candle shades, especially if they are made of card. In the wrong hands they could be a fire hazard, so take extreme care when the candle flames are alight. It is important that shades are held safely in place above and away from the flames. Use special metal shade holders which will keep them at a constant height above the flame as the candle burns down. Paper shades must fit correctly on the holders – look for ones with bevelled tops on which the shades will sit firmly. Holders can either sit on the candle or clip on it from the side. Always make sure that a small rim of metal shows above the top edge of the shade. You should also choose straight-sided candles with a high stearin content. The composition of other candles allows the wax to soften easily, and as the metal holder becomes hot the candle will start to lean dangerously. As always, never leave lit candles unattended and particularly if they have shades.

Opposite: *There is no limit to the different ways paper shades can be decorated to complement colourful candles.*

YOU WILL NEED

paper and pencil for template
scissors
thin card (posterboard)
various items, depending on type of shade: hole puncher; cord; large-eyed darning needle; spray paint; PVA (white) glue; fabric plus pins; needle and cotton; paper fasteners (paper clips); craft knife; knitting needle; silver pen; gingham ribbon

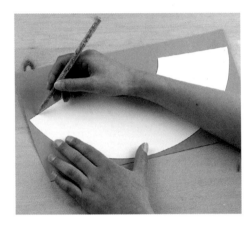

1 Size up the template on page 156 and draw round it on to coloured card. Cut out the shade.

2 To make a shade trimmed and held together with cord, first draw lightly in pencil all around the shade just a few millimetres in from the edge. Using the line as a guide, punch holes at regular intervals around all the sides.

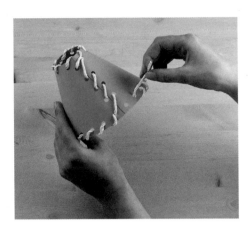

3 Fold the card into the shape of the shade. Thread a length of cord through one of the holes at the top, near where the card meets, and knot it on the inside. Work round the shade, looping the thread through all the holes, finishing with another knot on the inside at the bottom.

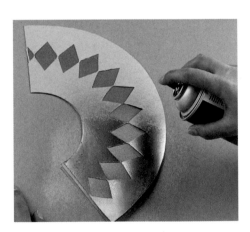

4 To decorate a shade with a repeating pattern, cut a second shade template out of paper or card. Draw your design on to this template and cut out the shapes which are to be painted to make a stencil. Place the stencil exactly over a shade cut out of card. Use spray paint to transfer the pattern on to the card chosen for the shade. When the paint is dry, fold the card into the shade, gluing the edges together where they meet.

5 It is easy to make fabric rosettes to decorate shades. Gather a strip of material to form a circle, hold it with a pin and then sew it together. You can add a second, larger layer to go behind the first and fix them both to the shade, with a paper fastener forming the centre of the rosette.

6 To make a shade with three-dimensional petals, make a stencil of flower petals. Draw whole flowers and a few extra petals on the shade, and draw a scalloped edge. Partly cut out the petals and fold them out-wards, then use a knitting needle to make indentations. Then cut along the scalloped edge.

7 As a variation on the corded shade, punch holes along the top and bottom edges of the card. Draw sil-ver stars, or whatever design you choose, on to the card. Leave to dry and then glue the card to make the shade. When firmly dry, thread lengths of gingham ribbon through the holes to form decorative borders.

TEMPLATES

In order to enlarge the templates to the size that you require, trace the template from the book and draw a grid of equal-sized squares over your tracing. Measure the space where the shape is to go and then draw a grid to these proportions, with an equal number of squares as appear on your tracing. Take each square individually and draw the relevant parts of the pattern in the larger square. Alternatively, you can enlarge your tracing on a photocopier if you have access to one.

Copper sconces, page 132 and fancy candle collars, page 151

Foil leaf chandelier, page 120

Papier-mâché leaf candleholders, page 142

Candle shades, page 154

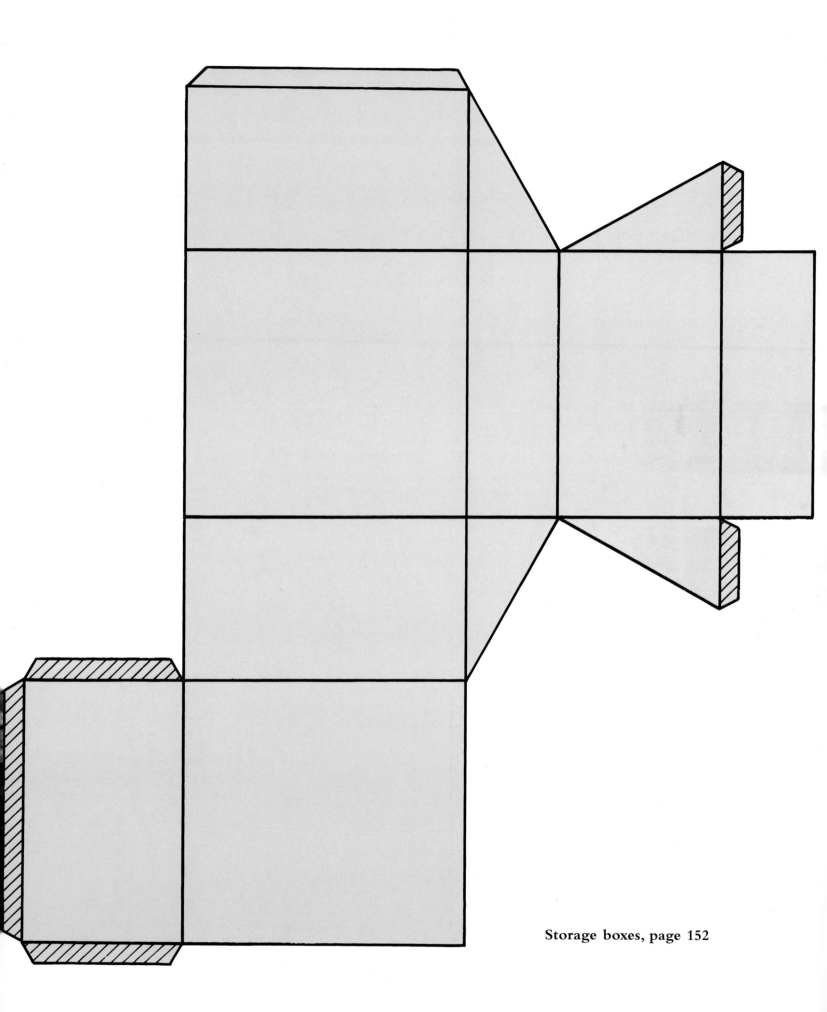

Storage boxes, page 152

SUPPLIERS

UNITED KINGDOM

Candle Maker's Supplies
28 Blythe Road
London W14 0HA
(020) 7602 4031
Everything you will need to make your own candles. Mail-order service with catalogue available on request

UNITED STATES OF AMERICA

Barker Enterprises, Inc.
15106 10th Avenue, SW
Seattle, WA 98166
(206) 244 1870
Candle-making supplies: dyes, waxes, glaze. Candle molds in over 650 shapes

CandlechemCo.
P.O. Box 705
Randolph, MA 02368
(617) 986 7541
Line of candle-making chemicals, scents, dyes, pigments, perfume, essential oils and others.

Candlestick
2444 Broadway
New York, NY 10024
(212) 787 5444
A wide selection of classic and novelty candles. Paraffin, beeswax and molds, scents and dyes also available

Dick Blick
P.O. Box 1267
Galesburg, IL 61402
(309) 343 6181
General craft supplier. Catalog available $4.00

Pottery Barn
Mail Order Department
P.O. Box 7044
San Francisco, CA 94120–7044
(800) 922 5507
Mail order catalog features various shapes and sizes of candles, candlesticks, and stencil kits, patinas and crackle glaze. There are also stores in major cities nationwide

Pourette Manufacturing Inc
681 Roosevelt Way NE
Seattle, WA 98155
(206) 525 4488
800–800–WICK (9245)
Candle-making supplies

CANADA

Charlotte Hobbys
782 Shield Road
Hemmingford
Quebec JOL 1HO
Canada
(516) 247 2590
Kits and candle supplies

AUSTRALIA

The Craft Company
272 Victoria Avenue
Chatswood NSW 2067
(02) 413 1781
Waxes, wicks, dyes and moulds

Hornsby Beekeeping Supplies
63a Hunter Street
Hornsby NSW 2077
(02) 477 5569
Bulk and coloured wax, and wicks

Janet's Art Supplies
145 Victoria Avenue
Chatswood NSW 2067
(02) 417 8572
Candle-making kits and beeswax

John L. Guilfoyle Pty Ltd
772 Boundary Road
Darra QLD 4076
(07) 375 3677
Sheets of pure beeswax, sheets of coloured beeswax, bulk beeswax and candle wicks

John L. Guilfoyle Pty Ltd
23 Charles Street
St Marys NSW 2760
(02) 623 5585
(as above)

John L. Guilfoyle Pty Ltd
299 Prospect Road
Blair Athol SA 5084
(08) 344 8307
(as above)

John L. Guilfoyle Pty Ltd
(09) 274 5062
(as above)

Mr Craft
Coolung Lane
Eastwood NSW 2122
(02) 858 2868
Paraffin wax, wicks, colours, moulds and books

NEW ZEALAND
Askew
(09) 358 1825
Bedingfields
(09) 367 6881
Bloomsbury Galleries
(09) 357 0889
Corso De Fiori
(09) 307 9166
Country Road Homewear
(03) 366 7870
French Country Collections
(09) 634 7230
Sanderson
(09) 309 0645
Gondwana International
(03) 477 6909
Marr Antiques and Interiors
(09) 309 7787
Indigo
(09) 302 0737
Levene
(09) 274 4211
Masterworks Gallery
(09) 309 5843
Makurm Textiles
(09) 379 3041
The Design Merchants
(09) 303 3188

ACKNOWLEDGEMENTS

The publishers and author would like to thank all the following companies, shops, suppliers and importers for their generosity in loaning items for photography.

CANDLE COMPANIES

Price's Patent Candle Company Ltd
110 York Road
London SW11 3RU
(020) 7228 3345
Wide range of candles and accessories, in particular a large number of church candles

Point à la ligne
Michael Johnson (Ceramics) Ltd
81 Kingsgate Road
London NW6 4JY
(020) 7624 2493
Exquisite shaped candles, accessories and modern ceramic candlesticks

Bougies La Française
UK subsidiary
LDX Marketing Ltd
19E Grove End Road
London NW8 9SD
(020) 7266 5000
Wide range of beautiful moulded candles and accessories

Arco
25 Calvin Street
London E1 6NW
(020) 7247 8847
Beautifully packaged church candles embossed with Roman numerals which indicate how long they will burn for

Kirker Greer & Co
Belvedere Road
Burnham-on-Crouch
Essex CM0 8AJ
(01621) 784647
Rolled beeswax candles in all shapes and sizes in natural and cream colours

Candlewick Green
Units 1 & 2 Donnington Park
Birdham Road
Donnington
Chichester
West Sussex PO20 7DU
(01243) 533277
Themed candles

CANDLE SHOPS

Angelic
6 Neal Street
London WC2H NLY
(020) 7240 2114
Wide range of candles and accessories

ACKNOWLEDGEMENTS

The Candle Shop
30 The Market
London WC2E 8RE
(020) 7836 9815
Wide range of candles and accessories

MATERIALS

Pebeo
Philip & Tacey
Northway
Andover
Hampshire SP10 5BA
(01264) 332171
Stained-glass paints

Plastikote Ltd
London Road Industrial Estate
Sawston
Cambridge CB2 4TR
(01223) 836400
Spray paints

SHOPS

The Dining Room Shop
62–64 White Hart Lane
London SW13 OPZ
(020) 8878 1020
Antique pressed glass candlesticks

Verandah
15b Blenheim Crescent
London W11 2EE
(020) 7792 9289
Tinware candlesticks and ethnic glassware

Sebastiano Barbagallo
15–17 Pembridge Road
London W11 3HG
(020) 7792 3320
Ethnic painted wood and metal candlesticks and holders

Past Times
Witney
Oxford OX8 6BH
(01993) 779444
Reproduction period candles and holders

Graham & Green
4 & 7 Elgin Crescent
London W11 2JA
(020) 7727 4594
Wide selection of contemporary and ethnic candles and holders

Neal Street East
5–7 Neal Street
London WC2H 9PU
(020) 7240 0135
Wide selection of candles and candleholders

Nice Irma's
46 Goodge Street
London W1P 1FJ
(020) 7580 6921
Imported ethnic candleholders and some contemporary kinds

Shaker
25 Harcourt Street
London W1H 1DT
(020) 7724 7672
Tinware and beeswax candles

Paperchase
213 Tottenham Court Road
London W1P 9AF
(020) 7580 8496
Ethnic candlesticks and accessories

Purves & Purves
80–81 & 83 Tottenham Court Road
London W1P 9HD
(020) 7580 8223
Candles and candlesticks

Janet Fitch
25a Old Compton Street
London W1V 5PL
(020) 7287 3789
Candlesticks made out of cutlery

Mildred Pearce
33 Earlham Street
London WC2H 9LD
(020) 7379 5128
Contemporary ceramic candlesticks

Avant Garden
77 Ledbury Road
London W11 2AG
(020) 7229 4408
Candles and candlesticks for the garden

Aero
96 Westbourne Grove
London W2 5RT
(020) 7221 1950
Modern wooden candlesticks

Gore Booker
41 Bedford Street
London WC2E 9HA
(020) 7497 1254
Candlesticks and chandeliers

MANUFACTURERS AND IMPORTERS

Diane Flint
84a Moray Road
London N4 3LA
(020) 7263 5405
Hand-crafted pewter candlesticks

Junction Eighteen
Bath Road
Warminster
Wiltshire BA12 8PE
(01985) 847774
Ethnic candleholders and storm lanterns

Hilary Lowe (available from)
George Clark
The High Street
Stockbridge
Hampshire
(01264) 811044
Period-style glass and silver candleholders and scented container candles

Global Village
17 St James Street
South Petherton
Somerset TA13 5BS
(01460) 241166
Fine selection of ethnic candleholders in metal and wood, including chandeliers

Golfar & Hughes
Studio C1
The Old Imperial Laundry
71 Warriner Gardens
London SW11 4XW
(020) 7498 0508
Manufacturers and designers of tôleware – range includes painted metal flower candlesticks and flower baskets

Poole Pottery Ltd
Poole
Dorset BH15 1RF
(01202) 666200
Manufacturers of fine tableware with candlesticks included as part of some design ranges

Royal Creamware
Junction 31
M62 Motorway
WF6 1TN
(01924) 898881
Reproduction creamware from original eighteenth-century designs – candlesticks included as part of range

Mary Rose Young
Oak House
Arthurs Folly
Parkend
Nr Lydney
Gloucestershire GL15 4JQ
(01594) 563425
Contemporary potter, making brightly hand-painted designs which includes candlesticks

William Sheppee Ltd
1a Church Avenue
London SW14 8NW
(020) 8392 2379
Wide range of metal candlesticks, candelabra, sconces and chandeliers

Yilmaz Uslu
Flat 8, 21 Seymour Street
London W1
(020) 7262 2504
Hand-made silver candlesticks

ADDITIONAL CREDITS

Additional thanks to the following: Thomas & Wilson, for the loan of plaster mouldings (020 7381 1161); Aynsley China Ltd, for loan of fine bone china cups and saucers (01782 599499); Yorkshire Fittings Ltd, for supplying plumbers fittings for candlestick project (0113 270104); Tobias and The Angel for loan of hyacinth glasses (020 8878 8902).

CONTRIBUTORS

Penny Boylan, p 116; David Constable of Candle Maker's Supplies, Gelligroes Mill, Gelligroes, Pontallanfraith, Blackwood, Gwent, pp 76–79, 82 and 100–101; Marion Elliot, p 92; Lucinda Ganderton, pp 130–131 and 148–149; Emma Hardy, pp 88–89, 118–119, 122–123, 150, 152–155; Mary Maguire, pp 58, 93, 96–97, 126–127, 132–133 and 136–141; Deborah Schneebeli-Morrell, pp 55, 86–87, 120–121, 142–145 and 151; Terry Moore, pp 128–129; Deborah Alexander p 134–135 and Sandra Rangecroft, Forever Flowering, Orchard House, Mortlake Road, Surrey TW9 4AS, pp19, 28 and 29.

Below: *Candle accessories.*

INDEX